HELD ACCOUNTABLE

HELD ACCOUNTABLE

•

GAIL MACMILLAN

AVALON BOOKS
NEW YORK

c. 1

PRINTED IN THE UNITED STATES OF AMERICA
ON ACID-FREE PAPER
BY HADDON CRAFTSMEN, BLOOMSBURG, PENNSYLVANIA

To my friends Eugenie, Gerry, Laura, Norma, and Shirley Ann:
Life without friends would be like a spring without flowers.

Chapter One

" "No need to worry, boys. They only sent a little blond chick to check the books. She can't be more than nineteen, a real high school girl. The boss will have a good laugh when he sees her."

As the mechanic's words drifted back into the cluttered office behind the hangar, Carol felt herself bristle. Bent over the scarred desk amid piles of disorganized scraps of paper, glasses perched on her pert nose, blond hair scraped back into a ponytail, Carol MacIntosh, Chartered Accountant, was not in the mood to take any guff from these men, whether they were mechanics or pilots in this ragtag squadron.

When the prestigious Toronto accounting firm where she was employed had been asked to audit the books of this small flying school in New Brunswick, the company had at first rejected the assignment. The Angus MacDonald Accounting Agency was not in the habit of taking on cases of suspected petty larceny, Janice Nickerson, its CEO, had declared. Hers was a highly reputable firm. Its most recent success had involved ferreting out a complex embezzlement scheme at a computer training facility in that same province, an accomplishment so innovatively clever it had made headlines in several national dailies and earned the gratitude of the provincial government.

Again the finance company that held the mortgage on the airfield had asked Ms. Nickerson to investigate, and again she had refused. A good bookkeeper could easily scrutinize the finances of such a small operation, she had argued. There was no reason that she could see to call in the heavy artillery to blow away a dust speck.

Then she had received another call. This time it was from the CEO of a huge conglomerate. The finance company came under their umbrella of control and thus the air school's viability as an investment. They would appreciate Ms. Nickerson's accepting the assignment for, small though it appeared, it was currently of major importance to them.

After another hesitation, she decided to take it on. It would be a good chance for her newest employee Carol MacIntosh to get her first field experience at investigative work on her own. For the past two years since Carol had received her Chartered Accountant's designation, Janice had kept her tied to a desk in the firm's Toronto offices. She knew, however, that she would someday have to give her young employee a chance to fly on her own and, when she had paused to consider it, this little airfield assignment seemed made to order.

"It's perfect for you and your experience level," Janice Nickerson informed her slender, golden-haired, twenty-seven-year-old CA. "Not difficult, but apparently extremely important to the consortium. Every penny of income and expenditure must be accounted for. James Caremore of Baycom believes there has been gross mismanagement of funds at the school and that even under new ownership, the operation just wouldn't be viable, located as it is miles from highly populated areas. Baycom is not famous for supporting losing concerns but always provides hard evidence to support its closure decisions to the local communities.''

Carol was elated. Here, early in her career, was a chance to make a name for herself with no senior accountant peering over her shoulder. And as a bonus, she would be out of the office for a couple of weeks. Lately she had begun to feel stifled by windowless rooms, computers that never took a break, fax machines that couldn't stop spewing out paper, and telephones that kept demanding immediate attention.

''I will caution you, however, to be aware of the reputation of the man who operates the flying school—the owner, in fact,'' her employer continued, opening a manila folder on her desk. ''Apparently during his teen years he was something of a rebel, with the looks of James Dean. He even drove a Harley-Davidson. High school girls worshiped him; their parents cursed him. His own parents, both commercial airline pilots, despaired of reforming him after he was expelled from private school here in Toronto and shipped him off to his grandfather who owned an airfield in New Brunswick.

"The grandfather apparently effected a miracle of sorts. After a few months of rampaging, the young man settled down. He became a licensed pilot and when his grandfather developed a heart condition, took over operation of the charter business and flying school. When Robert Bishop died, Jason, or Jake as he's known, inherited the place and kept it going."

"If he's so entirely reformed, then what's the problem?" Carol couldn't grasp the significance of all this background information.

"Carol." Janice Nickerson's voice softened from employer instructive to personal concern. "Jake Bishop is reputed to be handsome, charming, and without a fearful or shy bone in his body. I don't want to catapult you into a situation where, if you'll excuse my bluntness, you could be highly vulnerable just now."

"What are you talking about?" Carol

looked squarely across the wide oak desk at her employer and tried to appear surprised.

''This restlessness, this desire for adventure you've been expressing lately, is so unlike you.'' Janice Nickerson arose and came to look down at the young accountant, concern furrowing her forehead. ''You've always been one of the most organized, predictable, goal-oriented people I know. I thought you and John Martin were well on your way to a serious relationship, perhaps even setting up an accounting firm together. Then, suddenly, everything is changed. You break up with John, start taking self-defense classes—''

''John's old news,'' Carol broke in, getting up to face her slender, youthful-looking employer. ''He was tall, dark, handsome, and incredibly dull. I couldn't have lived my life in partnership with someone whose idea of adventure was walking barefoot across his living room carpet!''

''That's exactly what I mean,'' Janice Nickerson replied. ''Lately you've been looking for something this job and a quiet, sensible man like John Martin can't offer. Given your current state of mind you could be highly vulnerable to the charms of a swashbuckler like Jake Bishop.''

"Swashbuckler? Janice, I love it when you speak archaically!'' Carol was laughing. "He'll be a client, nothing more. For heaven's sake, how could you possibly for a moment believe that I might get involved with a back-woods pilot with a nearly bankrupt airfield and a silly fifties reputation? It'll be a lark, nothing more than a lark, to use some of your hopelessly outdated terminology!''

"Well, not too great a lark that you forget your reason for going to Bishop's Airfield, I hope,'' her employer said, returning to her desk and the manila folder. "According to this information there is a young man associated with the business who is the proverbial pillar of the community and can help you do just that. His name is Wade Jenkins, Jake Bishop's lawyer. And while he may not be able to help you with the financial aspects of Bishop's Airfield, James Caremore has assured me Mr. Jenkins will be able to help familiarize you with the operation. Look him up as soon as you get there.''

Four days later Carol was driving her rental car from Moncton, the nearest city with a commercial airport, to Riverbay, the small town located four miles from the airfield she was to audit. The temperature of the late June day must have been nearing the eighty-degree mark, she estimated. Pushing a damp strand of hair back from her forehead, she wished she hadn't been ruled by the intensely frugal side of her nature when she had rented a car earlier that morning. She should have taken the one with air-conditioning.

As she checked the map spread out on the seat beside her she noticed the highway she was on ran past the airfield just before it by-passed Riverbay. *I may as well get right to work*, she decided. *I'll go directly to the airfield, call from there to confirm my reservations at the Wiltsons' Bed and Breakfast in town, and get in a few hours' work before I actually show up on their doorstep. I can save the firm a half day's expenses that way.*

When the airfield came into view to the left of the highway, Carol was amazed by its vastness. She had been expecting a single dirt runway running along a swath cut into the forest. This definitely was not the case.

Acres and acres of cleared land stretched out before her with two long paved runways cutting straight black roads across the freshly mowed grass. Visibility for seemingly miles in all directions was unimpaired on the pancake-flat tableland.

Far at one end, shimmering like a mirage in the heat, was a dilapidated airplane hangar, its paint peeling, with a glassed-in box of a room on the roof she assumed was a control tower. Stuck to one side of the hangar was some sort of shack.

A few broken cement foundations nearby gave clues to the fact that the airfield had once been a much more extensive operation, and Carol recalled from research she had done before setting out on this audit that it had been an important training facility for British pilots during World War II. After hostilities had ceased, Robert Bishop, Jason's grandfather, a much-decorated fighter pilot, had purchased it. He had opened a civilian flying school and charter business that had been reasonably successful until his grandson had taken it over several years ago. Carol wondered what had caused this change in finances and knew it would be part of her job to find out.

As she turned off the highway, a faded sign informed her that she was now entering Bishop's Airfield. She recalled the inventory and staffing as given to her in the manila folder Janice Nickerson had handed her after she had finished warning her against the owner and recommending the attorney Wade Jenkins.

According to the document, only the hangar was in use; all other buildings had been de-molished as they fell into disuse and disrepair. There were only three aircraft: a Piper Cub used as a trainer, a King Air B200 nine-passenger charter craft, and a Sopwith Pup, whatever that was. The entire staff consisted of two people: Jason Bishop, owner, instruc-tor, and pilot; and Sam Hawkins, mechanic and air traffic controller.

Carol had shaken her head at this last job description. A mechanic who doubled as air traffic control . . . what kind of operation was Bishop's Airfield, anyway? she wondered.

She found out in short order. Her first

glance into the cluttered office that was the shed she had seen in the distance tacked to the disreputable excuse for a hangar, however, instantly gave her a disheartening overview of exactly what it was. It also explained why she had been given the assignment. It was a test, her employer was testing her, and this job looked like it would turn out to be the granddaddy of all exams.

Papers were scattered over the surface of a big, scarred desk, thumbtacked to the raw-beamed walls, and spread over the top of a couple of dented file cabinets; more were piled in untidy heaps on the dusty plank floor. A single, large window that gave a view of the runway, parking lot, and road leading up to the airfield housed the biggest spiderweb she had ever seen.

"Jake is flying in an air show in Nova Scotia today," the gnarled, gum-chewing figure in coveralls had explained as he led her across the echoing hangar where two gleaming white planes, one small, the other larger, sat idle. "Doesn't know what fear is, I guess. Otherwise he wouldn't be flying that antique he's up in right now, showing the crowd what old-time barnstorming was really like. And all because he needs money to keep this place open.'' He looked bitterly in Carol's direction, but she had stopped listening.

In a state of shock, she had been advancing into the cramped, filthy little room, briefcase suddenly desperately heavy in her hand. So this was the office, her place of work for the next two weeks. Hot and tired from her trip, she had felt like moaning long and loud over the dirt and disorganization that greeted her. But she hadn't. That would have been beneath both her dignity and sense of professionalism.

Instead, suddenly aware of the mechanic's amused, curious stare, she had thrown her briefcase on top of the desk, snapped it open, pulled out an elastic band, and tied her shoulder-length hair back into a ponytail. Then, putting on her glasses, she had sat down in the worn oak captain's swivel chair behind the desk and set to work.

A half hour later she paused to fan herself with a dog-eared file folder and grimaced as she glanced down at her once immaculate business attire. He silver-gray linen suit was smudged with dirt, her matching pumps covered with dust. *I might as well be working in a coal mine,* she thought disgustedly.

The intense heat didn't help. It had to be at least ninety degrees in the cramped little cubicle. There was no air-conditioning or even a fan to ease the stifling temperatures. Panty hose and blouse clung to her body in a sea of perspiration. Tomorrow, she vowed, it would be a cotton sundress and sandals for this chartered accountant.

She flipped open another soiled ledger and wrinkled her nose as she looked down at its cramped, grease-smudged figures. Then, reminding herself that a journey of a thousand miles starts with a single step, she sighed and set to work. Her fingers flamencoed over the keys of the ancient adding machine she had found peeping out from under a pile of papers on one corner of the desk, and totals rapidly began to appear.

It was a crude but effective device, she decided. And a good thing, she thought ruefully, since it was the only viable piece of technology in the office. The vintage, grime-covered computer perched precariously on a wobbly typing table in one corner was hopelessly ob-

solete and totally incompatible with any pro-
grams she was aware of. She wished she had
brought her laptop, but then she hadn't, in her
wildest dreams, imagined anything like the
situation she was confronting.

Lack of technical support wouldn't stop
her, however, she decided stubbornly. Carol
MacIntosh was out to prove herself, and the
more difficult the circumstances under which
she had to do it, the greater the evidence in
her favor would be when she succeeded.

Little blond high school chick indeed! Angrily she took her compact from her purse and
snapped it open. The face that greeted her in
its mirror made her wrinkle her nose in dis-
gust. Yes, there it was again, she thought, that
fresh, innocent, country girl look so overpowering she couldn't have hidden it if she
had ladled on makeup with a palette knife.

Why couldn't she look aloof and coolly
professional like her beautiful employer? Janice Nickerson's polished good looks fairly exuded sophistication and cleverness. Carol, on
the other hand, except for the golden hair,
might have been a Debbie Reynolds look-
alike in any of the actress's early roles.

"The day that little piece of fluff finds a loophole in our bookkeeping, we'll be making snowballs in July, fellas," the mechanic's continuing appraisal wafted back to her. "No need to worry."

As the mechanic's friends left chuckling, Carol's compact closed with a sharp snap and she stuffed it roughly back into her purse. *Snowballs in July, is it?* she thought, furious. *Well, get out your skis, boys! There's definitely a blizzard on the way!*

"You're not the only one that can weave a web, Gertie," she said, looking over at the industrious spider in the window and giving her a name. "I'm pretty good at catching wily flies like Jake Bishop myself."

Chapter Two

The monotonous drone of some type of aircraft engine filtered into the hot little office and drew Carol's attention away from the tangle of papers before her. For the past two hours she had been sorting the conglomeration of receipts, invoices, past dues, and other bits and pieces of paper on the desk and still she had not touched the rest of the office. What had been estimated by Janice Nickerson to be a week's work was looking more and more like a summer project. She sighed and pushed a strand of hair back into her ponytail.

The approaching plane drew her attention again. This time she arose and walked over to the window to look out at the sky and runway. And gasped.

An ancient-looking single-propeller aircraft that looked like a relic from a silent movie was slanting downward toward the landing strip. Even at this distance she could see it had an open cockpit, its aviator clearly silhouetted against the stark blueness of the late afternoon sky.

Oh, no! she thought. *Someone is actually flying that thing! Whoever he is, he must be insane!*

"That's Jake now," the mechanic astonished her by explaining as he came to join her at the window. "He's probably the best biplane pilot in this country. He was even asked to be a stunt double in a movie once . . . filling in for one those guys women find so great looking . . . can't remember his name . . . they're all alike to me."

"And did he accept?" Carol was impressed and intrigued. That hadn't been in any of the notes Janice had given her.

"No," Sam said slowly, chomping on his gum and staring up at the open-cockpitted aircraft. "Bob, his grandfather, was sick at the time and Jake refused to leave him. Hey, way to go, Boss!" His weathered face lit up as the biplane suddenly nosed upward and flipped into a heart-stopping loop-the-loop.

Carol gasped. "How did he do that? *Why* did he do that?"

"How, I couldn't tell you. Jake's the pilot and he learned from his grandfather. Why . . . well, that's just Jake's way of telling me everything is A-OK."

A few seconds later the plane touched down at the end of the runway, hiccuped a little, then settled into a steadily slowing run along the paved strip to the hangar. There the pilot swung it about and proceeded slowly to the building's entrance where it came to a full stop.

Carol stepped out of the office in time to see a tall, athletic male figure wearing a skull-hugging helmet, goggles, and brown coveralls vault easily out of the cockpit. As the pilot landed on the ground, he pulled off his head-gear and threw a companionable arm about the shoulders of the thin, stooped mechanic who had gone out to meet him.

Carol felt her breath gasp in her throat. He was the handsomest creature she had seen in months, maybe years. No wonder he had been asked to double for a movie star. Quickly she took off her glasses and shoved them into her purse.

"How did it go, Boss?" the mechanic asked, squinting up at the taller man and wiping his hands on a rag.

"Terrific, Sam, couldn't have been better," he said enthusiastically. "And I owe it all to my great ground crew, namely one Samuel Hawkins."

"Aw!" Obviously both pleased and embarrassed, Sam shrugged off the congratulatory arm and the praise. "Anyone can tighten a few nuts and bolts, but it takes guts to take an old crate like this off the ground." Then his tone changed as both men became aware of Carol standing just outside the office door at the rear of the hangar.

"Accountant's here." Sam's voice lowered and changed to a disgruntled mutter. He jerked his head toward her. Leaving the couple to meet on their own, he ambled over to inspect the newly arrived aircraft.

"From Toronto, I've been told." The aviator didn't hesitate. He strode quickly across the hangar, hand extended in greeting. "I'm Jake Bishop. Sorry I couldn't be here when you arrived. Has Sam shown you around?"

He reached her as he finished speaking and clasped her dirty, perspiring hand in his cool, dry one.

"Carol MacIntosh," her lips replied, but her mind cried, *"Wow!"* as she looked up into eyes that were as clear and blue as the sky out of which the man had recently dropped. "I'm pleased to meet you," she continued, struggling to remain businesslike and ignore her inward awestruck admiration for this incredibly handsome, incredibly charming man.

"Likewise," he said, his eyes crinkling at the corners, his mouth curling upward at the ends.

Don't smile like that, she silently ordered. *Give me a fighting chance!*

She tried desperately to dredge up the mechanic's belittling remarks to help her stay aloof and cold but found that even they didn't help. After all, Jake Bishop was totally innocent . . . so far.

"I'm sorry about the clutter," he continued. "I'm afraid a secretary's salary isn't within my means. Sam and I try to keep things straight but, as you've no doubt already observed, we haven't been entirely successful." He smiled again, this time a little ruefully.

"I'm sure I can sort through it in time," she said. "I visited a flying club in Toronto just before I came to New Brunswick and gathered information on aircraft like the three I saw on your inventory . . . fuel consumption, depreciation, cost of maintenance, and the like. It may help me discover the source of your financial difficulties."

Out of the corner of her eye, Carol saw the mechanic's expression change from amusement to astonishment. *Ha!* she thought gleefully. *Mr. Nuts and Bolts wasn't prepared for a little blond chick who's done her homework.*

"Good for you." Jake Bishop demonstrated none of his employee's chagrin and even seemed pleased. "But I hope you discovered more than just the facts and figures of flight. I hope you were also able to get a glimpse of its excitement and romance."

He's being so nice, Carol thought. *Doesn't*

he realize I'm here on behalf of a company that is looking for a financial reason to close him down?

"You know I'm here on Baycom's behalf to audit your books?" she felt compelled to ask, deliberately ignoring his "excitement and romance" comment. It sounded dangerously close to the opening line of a personal discussion and she didn't want to get involved in anything like that.

"Of course," he said. "I've been expecting it for some time. When you borrow money and are having a difficult time repaying it, you have to expect your creditors to be curious. Would you care for a cold drink?" He indicated an ancient soft drink dispenser at one side of the hangar.

"No thanks," she replied as he strode over to the machine, took some coins from his pocket, and inserted them into a slot. "I have to be going. I'm staying at the Wiltsons' Bed and Breakfast and Mrs. Wiltson has kindly agreed to also provide supper if I'm at the house by five-thirty."

"I'll be leaving myself, then," he said, un-zipping his flight suit while the machine clinked and sputtered as it struggled to release a can. "Baron will be hungry and he doesn't have a great deal of patience once his belly starts to complain."

"Baron?" Carol asked, trying to keep her eyes focused on Jake Bishop's face and not on the snow-white T-shirt pulled tightly across his broad, muscular chest or the well-fitted jeans revealed as he peeled himself out of his coveralls. There was no way an inch could be pinched on that lean, powerful torso, she thought.

"My beagle," he replied, stepping free of his suit and capturing a can as it crashed into a bottom tray. "His registered name is Baron Manfred von Richthoven the Red, but I call him Baron or sometimes, when the situation warrants, the Baron. Do you like dogs?"

Temptation was being rapidly heaped on temptation so swiftly Carol felt giddy. Did she like dogs! She adored dogs. And her favorite breed was the beagle.

"I had a beagle all the years I was growing up," she said, and wished Jake Bishop hadn't chosen to slouch into that classic James Dean pose against the pop machine, a Coke in his hand. "His name was Brandy. He lived to be sixteen years old."

"Then you understand." He grinned, straightening up. "You can't mess with a beagle's needs and sensibilities. I'll walk you to your car."

"Thank you," she said, trying to sound and look cool and sophisticated. "I'll get my purse and briefcase."

As she turned and walked back into the office she hoped her face didn't bear any smudges from her hours in the grubby little office. *I bet I've got a huge black mark on my face,* she thought. *I'm always pushing my glasses back up my nose and my hands are filthy. And my hair must really be attractive in this stupid ponytail.*

She longed to take a quick glance at herself in her compact mirror but realized she was in his full view. She couldn't possibly open her purse and check out her appearance without his seeing her. And she definitely didn't want to give him the impression she was primping for his benefit. He was the subject of her investigation, for heaven's sake!

Instead she drew a deep waiting breath, forced a too-bright smile across her face, and returned to where he stood waiting for her in the middle of the hangar. Together they walked to the small parking area where her compact rental car waited beside an open Jeep.

"I'll try to spend some time with you tomorrow," he said. "I'm sure you'll have questions."

"Yes," she said, and wished he wouldn't be so agreeable. He was only making her job more difficult. But maybe he knew that, she thought suddenly. Maybe this was all a tactic designed to disarm her. Well, it wouldn't work.

He opened the driver's door of her car but as she turned back to say good-bye after putting her purse and briefcase inside, he drew a snow-white handkerchief from his pocket and touched it lightly to the bridge of her nose.

"You have a smudge." He grinned. "Compliments, no doubt, of my grimy office."

Carol slid behind the wheel, burning with embarrassment.

''Arrgh!'' she grated in imitation of Charles Schulz's Snoopy as she drove away. Beagles always have such appropriate ways of expressing their frustration, she thought.

Chapter Three

That shower had been just what she needed, Carol decided as she finished toweling herself dry. She slipped into a gauzy white nightgown and returned to her room. Sighing contentedly, she settled into a chintz-covered chair near an open window overlooking the front veranda roof at the Wiltsons' Bed and Breakfast.

Night had fallen while she was in the shower and now only a streetlight illuminated the walk, lawn, trees, and flower beds below. Carol found the semidarkness soothing after the bright, hot day and decided against turning on a lamp.

Glancing out at the street through the night-blackened leaves of the maples on the lawn,

Carol saw a familiar-looking pickup parked in front of her boardinghouse. Where had she seen that truck before? she wondered. Suddenly she remembered.

It was at the airfield. It had been the only vehicle remaining in the parking lot when she and Jack had left that afternoon. Since Sam Hawkins had been the only other person still there at the time, it had to belong to him.

Her recollection was vindicated a moment later when the screen door onto the veranda below squeaked open and she heard Sam's slow drawl as he spoke to George Wiltson.

"Sorry about this, George," the mechanic was saying. "But you understand why it has to be done."

"Yes, Sam, sadly I do. I just wish there was some other way. This is a nice town. I hate to see anyone leave here with a bad impression."

"Yeah, well, you can't have an omelet without breaking eggs, as they say. And this town needs to keep its omelet, if you get my drift. Good night, now. I'll see you soon. Tell Erna her strawberry shortcake was great, as always."

Carol saw the mechanic emerge from beneath the shelter of the veranda roof and amble down the walk under spreading maples to his decrepit truck. Shortly, with a grinding of gears, the old vehicle drove away. She was left in the gathering darkness to finish drying her hair and wonder what the two men had been talking about. Then she shrugged. They must have been discussing town problems, nothing that would concern her, she thought.

Curling her bare feet up under her, Carol settled back in her chair and let the balminess of the summer night envelop her. After the intense heat of the July day, the cool of the evening air was wonderfully soothing. Hushed and delicate with the scent of lilacs, it was a time ripe for romance and suddenly she caught herself wondering what Jake Bishop was doing this languid summer evening. *Stop it,* she ordered herself sharply. *He's business, pure business.*

Then, through the gently undulating black lace shadows of the maples on the lawn below, she saw a young couple strolling slowly along the sidewalk. The girl wore a calf-length flowered skirt with a wide belt and flat ballerina-type shoes. Her long hair was held back with a velvet ribbon. The young man wore jeans and a white T-shirt and made Carol wonder with how many girls Jake had wandered down these peaceful streets.

The pair presently below her were holding hands and gazing at each other with looks as tender and intoxicating as the blossom-scented air. When they drew closer, Carol recognized the young woman to be the Wiltsons' daughter, Kathy, whom she had met at supper.

At the gate the couple turned in and strolled leisurely toward the front veranda. Then, still just within Carol's sight, they paused and faced each other. For a moment there was silence save for the rumble of an eighteen-wheeler on the bypass and the light rustling of a tender breeze in the maples. Time seemed suspended in a place of loving gazes, the air galvanized with passions held caringly in check.

Finally the girl rose on tiptoes to touch her lips to the young man's for a moment as light and enchanting as the brush of a butterfly's wing. When she dropped to her heels once more, he backed slowly away from her, letting their fingers touch until both had reached arms' length. Then he turned and jogged away into the soft darkness of the summer night.

Carol heaved a sigh and arose to go to bed. That young couple had set all sorts of ridiculous fantasies about herself and Jake racing through her head. It was time to put a stop to such foolishness.

It was this town, the whole area in fact, that was to blame for her romantic imaginings, she thought. It was as wholesome and innocent as most communities had been in North America during the 1950s. And as had often been the case in such communities during that decade, Riverbay even had its own local "bad boy" in the person of Jake Bishop, who had miraculously reformed and become a model citizen.

It's like a time warp, she thought. *It's like all the old television series I've ever seen from the era. I wouldn't be surprised if I met Ward and June Cleaver with the Beaver and Wally in tow on Main Street.*

Then she remembered Sam's cryptic words. Something definitely was wrong in Riverbay, she thought, and remembered other stories that had come out of the fifties, like *Town Without Pity* and *Rebel Without a Cause.* Did this apparently idyllic little community have dark secrets to hide beneath its veneer of goodwill and innocence?

Get back on track, girl, she told herself as she climbed between cool, snow-white sheets. *Don't get lost in the fifties, especially not with a man like Jake Bishop. You'll be sorry if you do.*

She slept well and awoke refreshed at seven the next morning. Pausing by her open window on her way to the bathroom, she saw what looked like the beginnings of another hot, sun-drenched summer day. Cotton sundress, sandals, some kind of upswept hairdo, and definitely no panty hose, she decided, and continued into the bathroom humming contentedly.

When she went down to breakfast a half hour later, she found the beautiful old Victorian dining room deserted. Croissants, Danish, fruit juice chilled in a tray of ice, and coffee waited on the sideboard, however, and after glancing at her watch, Carol decided to help herself. She was just finishing an apple-cinnamon Danish when the door to the kitchen opened and Mrs. Wiltson came into the room.

"Good morning." Carol smiled as she greeted the attractive, gray-haired woman. "It feels like the beginning of another warm day, doesn't it?"

"Yes, it does." To the younger woman's surprise, Mrs. Wiltson's friendliness of the previous day seemed to have disappeared into a sea of nervous tension. She started to pour herself a cup of coffee at the sideboard, then seemed to change her mind. Instead, she turned to face the young woman at the table, her slender hands tightly clenched at her sides, her face pale and tense.

"Miss MacIntosh, you'll have to find another place to stay," she blurted out. "I can't accommodate you any longer." Then she turned back to the sideboard and tried to pour herself coffee with shaking hands.

"Can't accommodate me any longer?" Carol was shocked. "Why not? When my secretary called for reservations, you booked me in for two weeks. I have written confirmation."

"I know, but we're having water problems," the woman replied without turning back to face her guest. "Because of this hot weather, our well is nearly dry. There'll be barely enough for George, Kathy, and me. Having anyone else in the house just now is impossible. I-I'm sorry.''

"Well, then, I'll just have to find somewhere else to stay." Carol took a final sip of her coffee and arose. "I'll get my things and take them to work with me. I'll leave a check on the dresser. And thank you for a delightful, if brief, stay. I hope your water problems will be over shortly."

"Yes . . . thank you . . . I'm sorry.'' The woman turned and hurried back into the kitchen. She was very near tears, Carol realized, and wondered if there were more serious problems than a water shortage in the house. She hoped not. She sincerely liked Erna Wiltson.

Fifteen minutes later Carol climbed into her rental car parked in the Wiltsons' wide driveway and turned the key. For a moment the motor struggled to turn over, then died. She tried again. *Come on, come on,* she urged silently. *I don't need any more problems this early in the day.*

Each successive attempt, however, brought

less and less response and finally none. Exasperated, she jumped out of the car and very nearly into the path of an open Jeep careening into the drive.

Brakes screeched and a familiar voice yelled, ''Careful!''

Whirling, she saw Jake Bishop climbing out of the vehicle and hurrying toward her.

''Are you okay?'' he asked, concern coloring his tone as he reached her.

''I'm fine,'' she said, shaking her head in frustration. ''It's this . . . this thing doubling as a car that's not okay!''

''Won't start?'' he asked needlessly. ''Here, let me try.''

He held out a hand for the keys and with an annoyed sigh, she handed them over to him. Why did every man in the world think that all he had to do was touch anything that a woman couldn't make work and it would magically come alive? Perversely she hoped the car wouldn't start. She hated motors that sprang into life and computers that immediately rolled back on line at a male touch.

Her wish came true. The only sound the car

uttered was a click as the key turned impotently in the ignition.

"Hmmm." Jake Bishop's suntanned forehead furrowed as he stared at the dashboard. "Seems as if your battery is dead or your starter is on the fritz." He climbed out and looked at her from behind his sunglasses. "I'll have Sam drive in and get it going later. Meanwhile, climb in. I'll drive you to the office."

"Don't bother." Carol tried to sound nonchalant as she looked at the dusty Jeep. "I'll call a cab."

"A cab? In this town? They don't exist."

"How do people get around if they don't have a car?" she asked, astonished.

"They call a friend," he said. "So just consider me a friend and come along."

He started back toward his Jeep and she realized she had no alternative but to go with him. Not if she planned to get to work that day, anyway.

"Wait," she called, and reached inside her disabled car to crack the trunk. "I have luggage."

He came back and joined her as she started

to pull two suitcases and a carry-on bag from the back of the car.

"You're moving out?" he asked, surprised. "You don't like it here?" He waved his hand to indicate the big, homey-looking white house surrounded by towering maples, green lawns, and colorful flower beds. "George and Erna Wiltson have reputations as excellent hosts."

"It wasn't my decision," she said, struggling with the largest valise. "The Wiltsons are having water problems. Their well is almost dry."

"Their well?" He had taken one suitcase from her and grasped the second one still in the trunk by its handle but paused at her words. "That's strange. I didn't know the Wiltsons had their own well. Every home and business in this town that I know of gets their water supply from central artesian wells." He frowned thoughtfully for a moment, then shrugged and started toward his Jeep. "So much for my knowledge of the Riverbay water system. Come on. Let's go. I have a student at nine o'clock."

Annoyed at his takeover of the situation and

the fact that she had no viable choice in the matter, Carol picked up the small remaining case from the trunk, retrieved her purse and her briefcase from the front seat, and followed him. *Who does he think he is?* she thought. *Janice was right about this guy. He is a co-lossal macho jerk.*

He put her suitcases into the back, then took her small satchel and briefcase from her and placed them beside the first two. With that chore finished, he strode around to the passenger side and waited.

She joined him and looked apprehensively at the vehicle's height and dusty condition. Not exactly designed with a lady in a white flowered sundress in mind, she thought.

Jake Bishop seemed to guess her thoughts. Like a knight errant, he swept her a deep bow, then extended a hand. "Allow me to assist you into my humble conveyance, milady," he said and grinned.

Taking his hand, she felt his warmth and strength as his fingers enveloped hers. *Easy, girl,* she warned herself. *He's business, strictly business.* Then, with as much dignity as her full-skirted dress and the Jeep's height would allow, she let him assist her into the vehicle.

"Here," he said, reaching across her as she searched for the seat belt. "Let me help. This isn't like most safety restraints. It takes a bit of orientation to master."

As his lean, muscular body draped itself over her, Carol caught the light scent of aftershave and felt her insides suddenly develop flip-flops as his soft, golden-brown hair grazed her bare shoulder. She was relieved when he finally snapped the belt in place and straightened up.

"There," he said, smiling at her. "Safely tucked in." Then he jogged back to the driver's seat.

Less than a minute later, however, she was wondering at the wisdom of her decision to accept the ride. As they headed out of town toward the airfield and Jake brought his vehicle up to highway speed, the wind caught the full skirt of her dress and flung it upward with abandon. Mortified, she clutched handfuls of cloth and attempted to stuff the shameless garment into submission under her knees.

No sooner had she succeeded in subduing

her wily skirt than her carefully upswept hair-style decided to run amok. Long tendrils whipped free of their restraining pins and lashed themselves wildly about her face. For a few moments she tried to repair the damage, then, with a resigned sigh, gave up the fight.

Then, sensing he was looking at her, she glanced in his direction and caught him just as he was returning his attention to the road and struggling to suppress his amusement. Was there no end to her embarrassing moments with this man? she wondered, giving one last vain attempt to smooth her dress and hair.

A moment later her question was answered. Something sharp and painful hit her in the right eye. She cried out, clutching a hand to her face. Instantly Jake pulled over to the side of the road and stopped.

"What happened?" he asked, leaning over her.

"A piece of dirt in my eye, I think," she said, trying to minimize her discomfort. "It will be okay in a minute."

But he had already jumped out of the vehicle and was hurrying around to her side.

"Let me see," he said, swinging one long leg into the Jeep and bracing his back against the windshield so that he was directly in front of her. His nearness brought twinges of excitement racing through her. This man exuded masculinity as naturally as the Wiltsons' lilacs gave off their heady fragrance, she thought. *Go away, Jake Bishop,* she ordered silently; then just as quickly, *No, don't.*

"Really, it's nothing," she tried to protest, but he had already pulled a handkerchief from his pocket and taken her chin gently in one hand. "Look up," he ordered as he tilted her head up and back.

"There it is," he said, dabbing gently into her eye with the handkerchief, and the next moment she felt relief. He paused for a moment, still holding her face in his hand, and smiled down at her. "Okay now?" He patted away a tear that had trickled from the corner of her eye and smiled.

He was so close, his eyes looking into hers so intensely blue, Carol felt a myriad of sensations wash over her. If he had tried to kiss her then and there she knew she wouldn't, couldn't have stopped him.

Wow! Carol thought for the second time in as many days. *This guy is perfectly gorgeous, one-hundred-percent terrific.* Then she forced herself to remember her position in his life and pulled away. *Business,* she fought to think, *he's only business. He has to be.*

She was glad, Carol tried to tell herself, when he moved away and pulled open the glove compartment to take out a pair of sunglasses similar to his own.

"Here," he said, handing them to her. "I should have given these to you before we started. There's always stuff in the air that can get into your eyes when you ride in an open vehicle."

He returned to the driver's seat. Carol hesitated a moment, then put on the glasses.

"Ready?" he asked before pulling back out onto the highway.

Carol took her briefcase from the back and put it in her lap, tucked her hair back behind her ears, and adjusted the sunglasses.

"Ready," she said, and they were off.

Deciding there was no way to preserve her hairdo or her facade of unruffled businesswoman for the next few minutes, Carol relaxed and gave herself over to enjoying the ride. She had never ridden in an open vehicle before that morning and she was finding the experience exhilarating.

The warm wind splashed over her, awakening every inch of mind and body to the pure joy of the ride. She felt alive and vibrant and, happily, very far from the artificially climatized fourteenth-floor offices of the Angus MacDonald Accounting Agency. When they reached the airfield she would once more become the cool, in-charge professional she really was, she told herself. But right now she was content to be as devil-may-care as her companion.

Beyond the town, the countryside spread out emerald green and springtime fresh. Fields and trees appeared pristine and vibrant beneath a sky of purest blue. Only a few other vehicles shared the road and when they passed, their drivers waved a greeting to Jake. Smog, traffic congestion, and rude motorists appeared nonexistent in this quiet backwater, and Carol was discovering she liked the ambience.

When they arrived at the airfield Jake freed

her from the seat belt she still couldn't figure out and carried her bags into the office. Sam, leaning against the antique biplane, said nothing, but his expression spoke volumes. *He probably thinks I'm moving in to have more time to pick his and his boss's finances apart,* Carol thought as she placed her briefcase on the cluttered desk.

"Before you settle down to work, I'd like to show you around my aircraft," Jake said. "You should be familiar with my inventory."

"That might be helpful," she agreed, wishing she had had a chance to repair her appearance after the windy ride but seeing Jake meant immediately.

She followed him out into the echoing doom that was the hangar and up to the largest of the three aircraft housed here.

"This is my charter plane," he said, putting a hand on its gleaming white side. "She's the imperial princess of the fleet, a King Air B200 twin-engine turboprop that seats nine passengers. She cruises at 310 miles per hour and is capable of traveling fifteen hundred miles between fuelings."

He led her up the steps and into the cabin.

It was spotlessly clean and smelled of fine leather. The seats looked spacious and comfortable for an aircraft of its size, and there was even a refreshment bar to provide hot coffee and cold drinks for passengers. Carol was impressed.

"My grandfather bought her just before he died," Jake explained. "He had had an old twelve-seater but it needed updating and major repairs so he opted to sell it and buy new. After all, charters are major sources of income for Bishop's Field, and people these days won't travel in anything less than absolute comfort."

Then he took her into the cockpit. An astonishing array of dials and instruments greeted her.

"Do you know all about this?" she asked, indicating the control panel, astounded. She had never been in this part of an aircraft and it was totally intimidating to her.

"I'm supposed to." He grinned, and she realized he was joking. "Otherwise it might be difficult to get this baby off the ground and bring her back down again."

Once again, Carol was impressed, but this time by her companion.

"This is my training plane," he said a few minutes later as they stood beside the middle plane. "He's a Piper Cub; slow, easy to handle, and forgiving with student pilots. As you can see he's fitted with pontoons for amphibious landings. He's a great little workhorse and can give anyone new to small plane travel an unequaled feeling of flight. I'll take you up in him sometime. You'll enjoy it."

Carol didn't reply. She wasn't about to make any commitment to go up in this little scrap of an aircraft even though it appeared in excellent condition. Her quest for adventure wasn't that far advanced at the moment.

Then he turned to the third aircraft, the one he had arrived in the previous day, the one with the terrifying open cockpit.

"And this is an exact replica of a Sopwith Pup," he said. "Do you know anything about World War One aircraft?"

She shook her head.

"The Pup here was the forerunner of the model known as the Sopwith Camel, one of which was responsible for the elimination of the Red Baron,'' he explained. ''And while over fifty-four hundred were built and used during World War One, the Sopwith Pup was, in my opinion and my granddad's, a more maneuverable aircraft with superior speed and climb. That's why he had a Pup made when he decided to try old-fashioned barnstorming, that is, performing crazy stunts in a vintage biplane model with an open cockpit. Did you know it was a Sopwith Pup that made the first landing ever on a moving ship and paved the way for carrier-based landings?''

Again, Carol shook her head, enthralled with his wealth of information. Up until then, aircraft had only been a means of getting from one place to another to her. Jake Bishop had personalized them . . . given them character and purpose and uniqueness. Now as she looked up at the three aircraft, they were no longer mere bits of metal and other assorted materials welded together into vaguely bird-like forms. Each was a distinct entity, an integral part of Jake Bishop's work and life.

''Hey, Jake.'' A teenager clad in a baggy T-shirt emblazoned with the images of a rock band, torn jeans, a navy kerchief tied biker-fashion about his head, and a gold earring in one ear, came into the hangar, dirty high-tops flapping. "Ready to make like a bird, man?"

"Right away, buddy." Jake turned toward the young man and grinned. "Think you'll be ready to solo by the end of the week?"

"No problem, man. Cool. Let's leave this world behind."

"I'll see you later," Jake said to Carol. "My student is here. If you need anything just ask Sam."

"*He's* your student?" she couldn't help asking softly as the young man wandered out of the hangar toward the Piper Cub Jake used as a trainer.

"Yes. You seem surprised."

"Well, I thought flying lessons were expensive. . . ." she began.

"And he doesn't look as if he can afford them?" Jake finished, his tone suddenly cold. "He can't. But he also can't afford not to have them."

He turned on his heel and walked away, leaving her thoroughly perplexed. If that tough-looking kid couldn't pay for lessons, then why was Jake giving them to him? Surely he must know he needed every penny to catch up on bills; surely . . .

With an exasperated sigh, Carol gave up trying to fathom Jake Bishop. Picking up her purse, she went into the rudimentary washroom near the office to repair her hair and makeup. A glance into the crazed bit of glass that served as a mirror over the stained wash basin made her cringe.

Her hair was a limp tangle straggling down in bits and pieces from its formerly sophisticated do. But worst of all she was sporting a huge black eye where her mascara had run as a result of the tears that piece of dust had produced.

She grew warm with embarrassment. Jake Bishop must think her face was perpetually dirty and that she was in constant need of male assistance to keep her life in order, she thought. She would have to rectify that impression and quickly if she were to gain his respect for her as a professional.

Fortunately there could never be even a hint of romantic involvement between them, she thought as she began to repair her makeup;

otherwise, she would have been doubly humiliated.

She returned to the office and sighed as she surveyed the task ahead of her. It seemed an impossible clutter but she would, she could, sort it out, she told herself.

She glanced over at the window and saw that the spider's web had grown overnight.

"You've been hard at it, Gertie," she said, crossing the room to take a closer look. "And you've even had a bit of success," she continued as she saw a fly dangling in one corner.

At that moment, Jake's Piper Cub sped past on the runway, gaining speed until it reached the end of the paving and nosed smoothly up into the cloudless summer sky. And for a moment, Carol's heart rose with the little aircraft into the fresh air and sunshine.

"They look so free, taking off like that, don't they?" she asked the spider. And suddenly she knew she didn't want to see Jake Bishop trapped and hopeless like that fly in any web she might be able to weave.

Chapter Four

"Hello. Ms. MacIntosh, I presume?"

Carol looked up to see a tall, dark-haired man standing in the office doorway. Wearing a tan silk suit, coordinating striped tie, and immaculate white shirt, he was as impeccably groomed as if he had just stepped from the pages of some exclusive menswear catalog.

"Yes," she said, feeling at a decided disadvantage. She had no idea who the attractive stranger was or how he came to know her name.

"I'm Wade Jenkins," he said, offering a nicely manicured hand. "Jake's attorney."

"I'm glad to meet you." Carol arose, smiling, and accepted his greeting. "My supervisor said you'd be in touch. Perhaps you can help me sort through some of Mr. Bishop's accounts.''

''I'd like to oblige, but the truth is I have very little knowledge of Jake's finances,'' he said a bit ruefully. ''He employs me mainly to keep his insurance policies up to date, his licenses current, and any of the other legalities involved in his business straight. I'm afraid all this''—he spread out a hand to take in the cluttered office—''is a bigger mystery to me than it must be to you. Actually, I came here simply to welcome you and to ask you to have lunch with me.''

''Lunch? Is it that time already?'' Carol glanced at her watch and wondered where the morning had gone. She had managed to make visible progress with the desk. Now stacks of paper lay in folders in organized piles and she had even managed to wipe the desk's scarred oak surface clean with a damp cloth.

''It certainly is.'' He smiled. ''And it's too nice a day to stay holed up in this clutter. What do you say? Will you join me?''

Carol hesitated only briefly. She hadn't had a chance to buy anything for lunch on the way to work, and she had no idea where the nearest restaurant was. Moreover, spending a little time with Jake's attorney could give her a chance to learn more about the pilot.

"I'd be delighted," she said. "Just give me a minute to freshen up."

Ten minutes later she was ensconced in the deep, luxurious front seat of Wade Jenkins's white Cadillac. As the big car glided past Sam, who was getting out of his pickup in the parking lot, the mechanic paused for a moment and stared at the couple. Then he touched his forehead in a farewell salute and headed toward the hangar.

Sam would be sure to tell Jake he had seen her leaving with Wade Jenkins, she thought, and wondered how the pilot would take that bit of information. He had just left on his second lesson of the day when Wade Jenkins had arrived.

She felt a smile threatening to curl her lips as she remembered Jake's second student that day. It had been Kathy Wiltson, the pretty brunet Carol had seen returning to her parents' home at the bed-and-breakfast the previous evening. The nineteen-year-old was obviously as much enthralled with her handsome instructor as with flying. Carol had been thoroughly amused as she had watched him affect a combination father–big brother attitude toward the young woman. Jake, although definitely not vain, was well aware of his effect on the young woman and not about to let her entertain any fantasies about him and her. He kept making references to someone named Danny who, Carol concluded, was the young man she had seen with Kathy the previous night. Jake was making sure his student wouldn't forget her genuine significant other in favor of a fantasy relationship that could never be more than a friendship.

But for now, Carol thought, she must put Jake Bishop out of her mind and concentrate on the pleasures of the moment. The car's air-conditioning barely ruffled a hair in her redone coiffure and, removed from wayward winds, her dress behaved with ladylike demureness.

The car glided quietly back to town, then out onto a secondary road along the river. Conversation was polite and impersonal, very much the discourse of two businesspeople, but as the elegant car slowed to travel over a narrow dirt road, Carol felt a slight sense of uneasiness. Her companion seemed to become aware of her trepidations and turned to smile reassuringly at her.

"If you're thinking there's no restaurant along this road, you're right," he said. "Actually we're headed for a picnic site by the river. I thought it was much too pleasant a day to spend indoors so in the hope that you'd accept my invitation, I brought a lunch. Not disappointed, are you?"

"Definitely not." Carol returned his smile and inwardly breathed easier. After all, she didn't really know this man, respectable though he appeared to be. "Fresh air will be wonderful after that tiny office."

They stopped on a secluded knoll overlooking the river. Several picnic tables were scattered about an area of freshly mowed grass, but it appeared Carol and Wade Jenkins were the only ones planning to use the facility that noon hour.

"It's beautiful," Carol said.

"I'm glad you approve," he said, and got

out of the car to open the passenger door for her.

As Carol wandered over to take a seat at one of the tables in the shade of a massive oak, Wade Jenkins opened the trunk and took out a large wicker picnic basket and small cooler. He carried both to the table Carol had chosen and opened the hamper.

"I hope you're not expecting a gourmet meal," he said, taking out an ivory-colored tablecloth and spreading it over the boards. "I concocted this lunch with a little help from the local supermarket deli. It's the best I could do in this town." Distaste flavored his final words and Carol glanced up at him quickly, her eyebrows raising questioningly.

"You look surprised," he said, pausing in removing containers from the basket. "I suppose Jake has been filling you with that 'dear hearts and gentle people' theme he seems to think pervades Riverbay. Well, some of us would like wider horizons to explore; some of us haven't run wild coast to coast on a Harley-Davidson yet." His voice had been rising emotionally. Suddenly he seemed to become aware of the fact and stopped short.

"Sorry." He smiled a little sheepishly, and returned to emptying the basket of its contents. "I'm letting my frustrations show."

"Frustrations?" Carol asked as he opened a tray of cold sliced meats and set out another of vegetables and dip. "Don't you enjoy living here?"

"It's fine if you fancy a snail's pace and have the interest level of a ten-year-old." He shrugged. He added an assortment of cheeses and a package of crusty rolls to the food already on the table. "And you're not forced to stay."

"Forced to stay?" Carol looked up at him curiously. Sunlight filtering through the maple leaves was casting areas of light and shadow over her companion in changing patterns.

"Perhaps that's an unkind assessment of my situation." He opened the cooler and took out a frosted bottle of white wine. "I care for my mother, who has a serious heart condition and who absolutely refuses to move away from here."

"That's very altruistic of you," Carol said, impressed by the integrity of the attractive man pouring wine into plastic glasses beside her. "I'm sure your mother is grateful."

"It's my responsibility," he said. "Cold cuts?" He changed the subject as he placed a plate and utensils before her and offered the platter of meats.

As they proceeded with their lunch, Wade turned the topic of conversation to Toronto and its business opportunities. He seemed fascinated by each bit of information Carol had to offer, hanging on her every word.

The combination of good food, fine wine, and attentive company made Carol feel relaxed and mellow. She forgot the cluttered office and the reality that immediately after lunch she would have to begin looking for a place to stay, a task she had avoided all morning. She was accustomed to having an efficient secretary to take care of such matters.

"Tell me about Jake Bishop," she asked during a lull in the conversation. "You've probably known him for some time."

"Since we were teenagers," he said, and Carol saw his expression harden. "Since he came here to live with his grandfather, since he was the town bad boy with every high school girl swooning over him and every wild young man trying to emulate him.''

"But he's changed, hasn't he?'' Carol asked, watching closely for Wade's reaction.

"Changed? I suppose. At least that's what most people around here like to think,'' he replied. ''And he has . . . on the surface, anyway. The Harley-Davidson is gone and he doesn't hang out at the local dance hall on Saturday nights anymore.'' He paused, then continued, ''I'm sorry. I didn't mean to paint a negative picture of Jake. I consider him my friend as well as my client. And he has done some good for the town by working with troubled teenagers. He's actually managed to get a few their pilots' licenses and on the road to careers in aviation. It's simply that I've known Jake for years and can't really believe a dyed-in-the-wool wildman like him can ever reform . . . completely.''

He hesitated, then continued more slowly, choosing his words carefully. ''Ms. Mac-Intosh . . . Carol, please be cautious where Jake Bishop is concerned. He's dated women . . . a lot of women . . . over the years, none of whom he took very seriously. Don't let him charm you into any kind of relationship you can't handle.''

"I appreciate your concern, Wade," she replied. "But I'm a big-city accountant, hardly a pushover for a pretty face and a colorful reputation. I assure you Jake Bishop is and will continue to be simply another audit to me."

"I'm relieved to hear that," he said. "Jake Bishop is a law unto himself. You're probably one of the few women I've met I feel confident can handle him."

"Thanks, I'm grateful for your encouragement." She smiled, then glancing at her watch, continued, "I really should be getting back now. I have a full afternoon's work ahead."

"Of course," he agreed, and together they began to gather up the picnic leftovers.

Wade had just finished fastening the hamper when the sound of an approaching vehicle made them both turn toward the entrance of the picnic site. A moment later Jake Bishop's Jeep with the pilot himself at the wheel came careening into view at a speed much too fast for the narrow dirt road. Its driver braked to a dust-raising halt beside Wade's Cadillac and swung out of the vehicle.

"I've come to take Miss MacIntosh back to the office," Jake Bishop said, blue eyes rock hard and brooking no room for refusal. The amiable man Carol had known since her arrival was gone. This was the rebel, the man Wade Jenkins had just warned her against as being a law unto himself, a vital, dangerous man. And he set her pulses racing.

"In case you haven't noticed, Jake, I can provide her transportation," Wade replied evenly, but he stepped back a pace and clenched and unclenched his hands at his sides.

"Yes, you can," the pilot continued as he came to face the attorney squarely, and Carol was instantly struck by the contrast they presented: the sun-weathered, wind-blown, leather-jacketed bad boy in mirror sunglasses and faded, well-fitted jeans and the impeccably groomed lawyer in his exclusively tailored business suit. "But you won't; I will."

He took Carol firmly by the arm and started to herd her into the Jeep.

"Now just a minute . . ." she began to protest but she was suddenly swung off her feet, placed in the Jeep's passenger seat, and firmly secured in place with that cantankerous seat belt. Before she could make a serious attempt to free herself, he was in the driver's seat and spinning the vehicle around. Within seconds they were bouncing down the road away from the picnic site, leaving a disgruntled Wade Jenkins staring after them.

"Of all the high-handed, stupidly macho, inconsiderate . . ." Carol sputtered, struggling at her restraint.

"You're right," he astonished her by agreeing. "But your consorting with Wade Jenkins isn't a good idea and I don't have time to explain or argue the fact. I have a student in fifteen minutes."

"And that, in your mind, justifies that . . . that act of barbarism back there?!" Carol cried.

"Not really." He turned to her and grinned wickedly. "But every so often I have to polish up my infamous reputation. And admit it. Didn't you get a charge out of being carried off by the town rake?"

"You're incorrigible." She abandoned her

struggle with the seat belt as she felt her indignation melting and a reluctant grin overpowering her disgruntled expression. "Do you think my life is so dull I need your pathetic attempt at dramatics to enliven it?"

He shrugged. "Having lunch with Wade Jenkins smacks of a good, solid, deadly dull way for anyone to kill a noon hour."

"But he's your attorney, isn't he?" Carol gave up on the seat belt, tucked her dress firmly under her knees, and took the sunglasses from the glove compartment. "You don't seem to have a very high regard for him."

"He keeps my licenses and insurance policies current and he's supposed to take my part if there's ever an accident involving one of my planes," he said, concentrating on the road and continuing to drive too fast for conditions. "Since that constitutes the extent of his involvement with my business, there's no need for him to be meeting with the person auditing my books . . . at least not without me present. I'll tell you anything you want to know about my operation or me. All you have to do is ask."

"You don't sound very confident about him," Carol said, feeling her hair once more beginning to lurch free. Resigned to the hopelessness of retaining her hairdo this time, she pulled out the remaining pins and shook her style free. "Why do you continue to keep him on as legal counsel?"

"He's the only attorney in town under sixty years of age, the only one willing to represent someone with my . . . shall we say . . . colorful past?" He pulled his sunglasses down his nose for a second and looked over them at her, blue eyes crackling with humor.

"You mean your reputation as town bad boy?" Carol said, her hair frolicking about her face in the wind.

"Sort of," he replied, pushing his glasses back in place and returning his attention to the road as they entered the town and took a right out onto the highway that led to the airfield. "I take it Wade filled you in on the details?"

"He said you'd been a bit wild but that you'd apparently reformed!" She had to bring her voice up to a near yell as he shifted gears and brought the vehicle to highway speed. "Obviously he was being generous!"

Chapter Five

Carol was beginning to feel desperate. It was nearly 5:00 and she had not found another place to stay. Aside from the Wiltsons' there were only three other bed-and-breakfasts in town she had discovered and they were all, for various reasons, unable to accommodate her. To her further amazement she had learned there was not a single hotel or motel within fifty miles. Tourists who came to the area were either few enough to be put up at the four bed-and-breakfasts or sports fishermen who continued on up the river to one of the camps operated by local residents.

With an exhausted sigh she leaned back in the creaking captain's chair behind the newly organized desk and wondered what she would do. Maybe she could get a cot and a sleeping bag and somehow camp out here, she thought, looking about the cluttered little room. She could use the airfield washroom and eat at a takeout in town.

Then she remembered another disabling fact—she had no vehicle. In her concern about getting a place to stay, she had completely forgotten. Had Sam been able to fix it? She arose and went out into the hangar where the mechanic was busy straightening out his tools on a workbench.

"Sam, did you have time to look at my car?" she asked.

"Yeah, yeah, I did," he said in his usual slow, drawling fashion. "Needs a new starter."

"And how long will it take to replace?" she asked, a sinking feeling already taking possession of her stomach.

"Oh, no more than a week," he replied, casually turning back to his work. "I had the car towed out here and ordered the parts right off so I can start working on it the minute they come in."

"A week? I can't possibly be without a car for an entire week!" Carol couldn't believe she was having this much bad luck at one time.

"Sorry, but that's the best I can do." The mechanic returned to his work, humming an old country tune.

"Well, that's just dandy!" Carol threw up her hands in total exasperation. "I have no car and no place to stay! What am I supposed to do now?"

"You can come stay with me and I'll drive you to work."

Whirling, Carol saw Jake Bishop sauntering into the hangar, that horrible, irresistible grin disturbing the symmetry of his perfect features again.

"Stay with you! I think not, not after your Conan the Barbarian act at noon today!" Carol faced him squarely, hands firmly planted on her hips. "Not even if you live with three maiden aunts next to the police station!"

"I figured you were a smart cookie from the first minute I laid eyes on you." Sam ambled over to join the couple, wiping his hands, his face brightening with approval of her remarks.

Right, of course you did, Carol thought sarcastically, remembering his derogatory remarks on her arrival.

"Give me a break, Sam." Jake threw an annoyed glance at the mechanic, then continued, "Miss MacIntosh, I assure you I never have and never will take unfair advantage of any woman. At any rate, it would be crazy in your case. I don't need to incite the wrath of my auditor and drive her to even greater lengths to close me down. Rather, it's in my best interest to treat you with the utmost respect. I'd advise you to give my invitation careful consideration, since it seems that at the present moment, I have the only vacant room in town."

His eyes narrowed in warning as he looked over at Sam, and the mechanic, after a slight hesitation, shrugged his indifference.

"Go stay with him if you think you can," he said to Carol. "But Jake is the worst housekeeper I know. It'll take you a week just to find the kitchen table."

"All the more reason for Miss MacIntosh

to move in,'' Jake said, striding into the office.
He came out a moment later carrying her two
suitcases. ''The cabin can use a woman's
touch. And she's already told me she likes
dogs, beagles in particular, so the Baron is no
problem. They'll be friends in no time. Speaking of whom, he must be hungry.''

He headed out to where his Jeep was parked
and threw the suitcases in back.

''Well, hurry up.'' He waved her to him
with an impatient hand. ''Get your purse and
that briefcase full of incriminating evidence
and come on. Beagles' bellies wait for no
one.''

Carol gave herself a quick mental review of
some of the moves she had learned in self-
defense class and decided she could handle
the situation. She shrugged her indifference in
Sam's direction, then followed Jake Bishop to
his Jeep.

Jake's cabin was located on the bank of one
of the river's branches renowned for its
salmon fishing and at the end of a mile-long
drive from the highway through groves of
pines and birches. Shingled with cedar, it was
painted an environmentally friendly brown

with forest green trim. A wide, sprawling structure, it had a low-sloped roof that slid gently forward to cover a full-length screened veranda along its front. A lawn badly in need of cutting spread out about it briefly before being swallowed up by forest. It was peaceful and cool and beautiful, and very isolated.

Carol felt a shiver part pleasure, part excitement, part apprehension slide over her. She wondered what Janice Nickerson would say if she knew what her newest employee was doing on her first major assignment.

Jake came to unfasten the difficult seat belt. Once again he bent across her, once again the soft, golden-brown hair brushed against her bare shoulder. *I've got to master this seat belt,* she thought. *I don't know how much more of this I can put up with.* A slight shiver washed over her in spite of her best efforts to suppress it.

"What's wrong?" he asked, catching it and looking up at her in concern.

"I assumed you lived in town," she fumbled for an explanation. "This is a bit isolated, isn't it?"

"Yes, it is," he agreed. "But my grandfather liked it and so do I. It's a complete get-away from the noise, hot pavement, and fumes of the airfield, a great place to regroup after a hard day, Granddad used to say. Try it. You might discover you like it, too.''

He smiled reassuringly and offered his hand to help her out of the vehicle. Carol could only accept.

A wild, joyous barking erupted from the cabin as Jake took Carol's suitcases from the Jeep and headed for a closed-in porch at the side.

"Come on," he said. "As you can hear, the Baron awaits."

The first room they entered appeared to be newer than the rest of the structure, probably, added, Carol guessed, to house the washer and dryer it contained. Magazines, cardboard boxes, and newspapers were stacked high on both. Along one of its wallboard-paneled sides, brass coat hangers held an assortment of jackets and rain gear. Beneath, a boot tray struggled to contain a tangled collection of male footwear. The floor itself gave vindication to the popular name of mudroom for such a back entrance.

Ugh! she thought. Sam wasn't kidding when he said Jake was a bad housekeeper.

Apparently unaware of Carol's dismay, Jake shoved open the curtains at one end and looked out at the river sparkling past in the late-afternoon sun. He turned back to her and gave a resigned shrug as the barking from the other side of the door leading into the main house grew even more insistent.

"Okay, okay, I'm coming," he said as he inserted a key into the lock. "I lock this part of the house not to keep intruders out," he explained, "but to keep the Baron in. Someone might come to visit and accidentally let him out. Since you're familiar with beagles you know what that means, especially in a wooded area . . . hours of waiting and worrying while he pursues every rabbit within miles."

He pushed open the door and a black, white, and tan bundle of pure energy hit him at full speed.

"Easy, Baron, easy, chum!" He laughed, scooping the little dog up and giving him a hug. "I'm home. And I've brought you a new friend, someone who knows all about beagles and their wily ways. So mind your manners, buddy.''

Grinning, he turned to Carol, the ecstatic little dog, desperately trying to lick his face, tail flogging, still in his arms.

"Hello, Baron." Carol smiled in sincere delight. She went to put a hand on his velvety head. "I'm glad to meet you. Do you know you're a very handsome fellow?"

"Ever the ladies' man, eh, Baron?" Jake replaced the dog on the floor and Carol welcomed the reassuring feeling that had come over her as she had watched Jake with his pet. No man who loved and was loved by an animal could be all bad, she knew.

Wagging his white-tipped tail and looking up at her with a full measure of roguish beagle charm, the Baron immediately trotted over to Carol. She knelt and scratched him behind one of his long, soft ears, glad to have a dog to enjoy again.

"Careful," Jake teased. "Don't let him think he's won you over. He can be an arrogant furball if he thinks he's captured you with his canine charms. Come in." He continued pushing open the door and leading her into the kitchen area. "He'll be demanding food in a minute."

The mudroom had been a fitting prologue to the house, Carol discovered. The kitchen, which was a long strip running across the back of the cabin, separated from the living area by a bar divider, was littered with the boxes and bags left from takeout meals, its sink piled high with unwashed dishes. A doggie door at one end opened into what Carol could see through a window above it was a well-fenced run. The entire area smelled of stale food and musty air.

The living room beyond was no better. Awash with newspapers, sports magazines, junk mail, and an assortment of carelessly shed male clothing, it obviously hadn't seen a dustcloth or vacuum cleaner in a very long time. Couch, chairs, bookcases, and end tables were barely visible in the mess. Ashes from a huge fieldstone fireplace that dominated the right wall hadn't yet fallen victim to any spring cleaning, and the big glass doors that opened onto the veranda were streaked and fingerprinted. How could a man who always looked as freshly showered and military neat as Jake live in such a jumble? she wondered.

"Sam warned you I wasn't much of a housekeeper," he said, catching her expression and stepping quickly into the living room to retrieve a pair of boxer shorts hanging from a lampshade. He tried only half successfully to stuff them back into a back pocket of his jeans. "First thing tomorrow the Baron and I will tidy up. We weren't prepared for guests, as you can see."

Carol suppressed a smile and set her purse down on a sticky kitchen counter. The cabin, under all this mess, probably was a charming place, she told herself. The varnished tongue-and-groove boards on walls and ceilings were mellowed a rich golden hue with age, the wide floor planks painted gray told of an era when pines massive enough to provide them still grew along the river, and the big fireplace conjured images of intimate winter evenings before its warmth. Given a good cleaning, it could be a really nice place to stay... temporarily.

"I like it," she said.

"I'm glad," he said and smiled at her. "It belonged to my granddad."

He crossed the room to open a pair of garden doors that gave access to the wide, screened veranda. Refreshing pine-scented air and the soothing sound of the river lapping along the shore wafted into the cabin together with the golden rays of a summer sun sliding down through the early evening sky.

"Bob Bishop was a sportsman to the core," he said, spreading out an arm to indicate the numerous black-and-white photos scattered about the walls. They depicted pilots with their various types of aircraft, harness racing championships, and fishing parties with their impressive catches. "He lived life, every minute of it, to the fullest right up until he passed away five years ago. But I still miss him just as much as I did on the first day he was gone."

He paused and stood for a moment gazing out at the river gleaming in the late afternoon sun. And for the first time since she had met him, Jake Bishop seemed vulnerable.

"I know what you mean," she said softly. "My grandmother died several years ago. She lived in a small town in Nova Scotia. Brandy, my beagle, and I used to spend most of our summers with her when I was a child. She was Irish with a real thirst for adventure, and . . . very special.''

"Yeah, well . . .'' Jake lowered his head for a moment, then turned back to her with a faint smile. "I'll show you to your room.''

He wasn't ready to talk to her about matters that were close to his heart, she realized, as she followed him to one of two doors on the left side of the living room. It was just as well, she thought. Better not to get involved at all, in any way.

Jake opened one of the doors to reveal a small bedroom with a narrow, quilt-covered bed, four-drawer dresser of 1930s vintage, and a small mahogany nightstand that would have done well at an antique auction. Brass hooks along one wall served as a closet. A window at the rear looked out onto the yard near the back door. A thin layer of dust covered the floor and furniture and there was an odor of disuse in the pine-paneled cubicle.

"It's a bit musty,'' he commented, moving ahead of her to throw open the window and let in fresh, forest-scented air. ''But it will be okay in a few minutes.''

''Was this your grandfather's room?'' she asked a moment later when he brought in her suitcases.

''No, it was my room after I came here to live with him, my room until he died,'' he said, placing her luggage beside the bed. ''When he passed away, I moved into his next door. I told myself it was because it had a better view of the river, but that wasn't true. I just felt closer to him there. He was the best, the most positive influence in my life, and I needed his ongoing support. Sounds crazy, doesn't it?''

He ran a hand through his golden-brown hair and looked at Carol, searching for her reaction to his admission.

''No,'' she said softly. ''I carried my father's eyeglass case with me for years after he died. Each time I touched it, I felt he wasn't so very far away. Janice Nickerson, my supervisor, couldn't understand it, however. I guess she's too much the pragmatist.''

''So the CEO of the Angus MacDonald Accounting Agency is a hard-nosed businesswoman, is she?'' he asked. ''Not given to understand flights of fancy? That's not good news.''

''You know what firm I represent?'' she asked, surprised. She had believed he had thought she was simply an accountant sent on behalf of his mortgage holders and knew nothing more about her.

''Of course,'' he replied. ''I did a little investigating of my own when I found out I was to be audited with an eye to closing me down. When I learned your firm had been hired and its reputation for fairness and honesty, I felt a little better. With people like that going over my books, I knew I had at least a fighting chance.''

''I'm glad we inspire your confidence,'' she said, running a finger along the edge of the dresser and looking down at the dust she had picked up to avoid meeting his eyes. ''Our goal is to be fair to all parties concerned.''

''Well, good,'' he said, sitting down on the edge of the bed. ''I might just survive this audit after all. Now tell me about Carol MacIntosh. I could be very interested.'' His eyes lit up with that irresistible twinkle she was finding more and more difficult to ignore.

"No." She shook her head and turned away to feign interest in her hair in the dresser mirror. "We can't get personal."

"Oh, yeah, right!" Annoyed, Jake arose and started for the door. "I'll get dinner. The Baron will keep you company. Make yourself comfortable," he continued his tone, becoming cordial once again. "The bathroom is across the living room, behind the fireplace."

He went out and a moment later she heard his Jeep start. Another takeout, she guessed, recalling the mess in the kitchen, and sighed as she looked about the dusty little room. Well, at least it was a place to stay.

Baron had followed Jake to the door and begun to whine as he realized his master wasn't going to take him along. When the sound of the Jeep had faded away in the distance, the little dog lay down, his nose against the doorjamb, and yowled mournfully.

"Come here, boy." Carol went into the living room and called the beagle. "You can help me tidy up. Maybe I can even find your food so you won't have to wait for Jake."

The little dog hesitated a moment, then trotted over to her, tail wagging. She knelt and hugged him. It brought a flood of good memories rushing back into her mind and suddenly she felt wonderfully happy.

"I think we're going to be good friends, Baron von Richthoven," she said, cradling the little dog in her arms.

Chapter Six

By the time Jake had returned the kitchen table had been cleared, washed, and neatly set for two. Clean dishes stood drying in a rack by the sink. Carol, wearing jeans and navy T-shirt, turned to look up at the pilot from where she was crouched on the floor filling the Baron's bowl with kibble. She grinned a bit ruefully.

"I hope you don't mind," she said lamely. "The Baron was hungry. And"—she followed his gaze to the clean table and sink— "I needed a change from ledgers and figures."

"Mind?" He put the bags of chicken take-out on the counter, his face lighting up with pleasure. "This is great! But you didn't have to. I didn't invite you to stay here with the hope of getting free housework. I was joking when I said the cabin needed a woman's touch. First thing tomorrow I'll make this place fit for a lady."

"It was actually kind of fun." She opened a container of fried chicken, took an appreciative sniff, and realized she was ravenous. "With the Baron helping."

"Nevertheless, thanks," he said, snapping the plastic lid from a container of coleslaw. "No one enjoys living in a mess. I just haven't had time for housekeeping chores lately. Keeping the airfield afloat takes every waking minute."

He suddenly looked tired and worried. Carol felt a wave of sympathy wash over her, then quickly muffled it. *Don't let him get to you, don't, don't, don't!* she ordered herself.

"But I don't want to talk work tonight," he said, pulling himself out of his heavy thoughts and holding out a chair for her with a grin. "Let's eat. I'm sure it can't compete with whatever epicurean fare Wade had to offer for lunch, but it'll be filling." He sat down opposite her and offered her a container of potato salad.

Carol was amazed at how easy it became to relax and enjoy both the cabin's mellow ambience and her companion's easy conversation. After they had eaten and cleared away the remains of the meal, Jake suggested they take the Baron for a walk, and she readily agreed. With the little dog snuffling for rabbits in the bushes beside the trail, they took a footpath along the river's edge. As they walked they swapped beagle stories and enjoyed the Baron's antics as he tried unsuccessfully to catch a large frog. Both conscientiously avoided shop talk.

The sun was setting by the time they returned to the cabin. Carol felt a sense of utter peace and contentment she couldn't completely understand, but which she was beginning to suspect was connected to Jake Bishop's engaging presence.

"It's early yet," he said, as they mounted the plank steps to the screened veranda. "We could sit on the porch swing for a while if you like."

"I'd like." She smiled and sat down on one

end of the old swing that hung suspended from the beams of the veranda roof. "It's lovely here, so peaceful with the river practically at the doorstep and the trees whispering in the evening breeze and no noisy neighbors."

"It's like an oasis to me after the airfield," he said, sitting down beside her as the Baron flopped tiredly at his feet. "Flying is my job and I love it but I need this place with its peace, its quiet, its unspoiled beauty as a place to refuel."

"I understand," she said softly, and leaned back in the swing.

"My grandfather built this cabin for my grandmother when they got married in 1935," Jake said. "She was one of the few members of our family who wasn't enamored with aircraft. She didn't want to live anywhere near the airfield. Actually I think she didn't want to be able to see Granddad fly. It terrified her."

"She loved him," Carol said. "To think of him crashing, possibly dying, would have been too horrendous for her to contemplate."

"I guess so." Jake let out his breath slowly

in a sigh and stretched long legs in front of him. "It certainly doesn't bother my mother, Captain Molly Bishop."

"Your mother is a commerical airline pilot, I understand," Carol said, knowing she shouldn't be getting into personal subjects and yet curious to learn all she could about Jason Bishop.

"She was," he said. "She retired last winter and bought a house in a Toronto suburb to be near my paragon of an older brother, Michael, the neurosurgeon, his perfect wife, Linda, and my three extraordinary nephews."

"Do I detect a healthy dose of sibling rivalry?" Carol asked as his tone grew bitter and sarcastic.

"Yeah, well . . ." He glanced over at her and grinned sheepishly. "It's just that Mike was always held up as a glowing example of all I should aspire to be and the mighty measuring stick that indicated just how badly I failed to do so."

He drew a deep sigh, then continued.

"The whole thing came to a climax when we were both in high school at an exclusive private institution in Toronto. Mike, a year older than me, was about to graduate at the top of his class. Mom and Dad came to the ceremony. They praised Mike to the hilt for his accomplishments and gave me the dickens for my less-than-stellar academic performance, all in one action-packed half hour.

"It was the last straw." Jake's voice deepened with the pain of a profound emotional experience remembered. "I split . . . took the Harley-Davidson my parents had given Mike as a graduation gift and headed out, determined never to go back. By the time the private detective my father hired found me, I had been to Vancouver and had recrossed the country to end up in Halifax, broke and suffering from malnutrition."

He paused and looked over at Carol, trying to gauge her reaction.

"Go on," she said softly.

"For the first time I saw pain, actual pain in my mother's normally cool, professionally impersonal demeanor," he continued, looking down at his hands clasped between his spread knees. "And I felt just repentant enough and sufficiently at their mercy in my weakened condition to agree to their terms of surrender.''

''Which were?'' Carol asked, thoroughly intrigued by his story.

''That I go and live with Granddad here in Riverbay and clean up my act,'' he said. ''Mom and Dad felt Riverbay with its quiet, small-town values might help give me a sense of direction. After all, my dad grew up here and wasn't he, like Mike, perfect?''

Bitterness crept back into his voice and he stopped himself, shaking his head ruefully.

''Sorry . . . old wounds,'' he said, looking over at her sadly.

''The worst kind,'' Carol said gently.

''Agreed,'' he replied, then continued his story. ''I didn't settle easily into the Riverbay tempo. Gram had died the year before and I guess Granddad took me in partly, at least, out of loneliness. Sad to say I wasn't much help to him.

''Oh, I obeyed curfews and worked around the airfield for him but my parents, in the deal they had made to make me come here, had allowed me to keep the Harley. That was all I needed to set up my reputation as the town hoodlum. And I enjoyed it. For once, I was number one . . . girls chasing me, guys trying to emulate me, everyone half afraid of me. Then . . .''

He paused and arose to walk to the front of the veranda and look out at the river, twinkling in the light of a rising moon.

''Then?'' Carol couldn't help pressing. She was entirely caught up in his story.

''Then . . . Granddad had a heart attack . . . ended up as a semi-invalid.'' He caught angrily at a raw beam over his head and Carol saw the muscles in his back stiffen. ''I had to wise up.''

''That was when you took over most of the responsibilities of the airfield.'' Carol was piecing his story together.

''Yes. Fortunately I'd had enough sense to get my commercial pilot's license before Granddad became ill,'' he said, and turned back to her, shaking his head and smiling ruefully at the memory. ''Granddad had even taught me those old barnstorming stunts which have come in handy when money's been tight since he died.''

''Until your grandfather passed away, you

had no financial problems?'' Carol asked, suddenly finding his story was swerving into an area where she had professional interest.

''No, we didn't,'' he said honestly. ''Granddad did the books right up until a week before he died.''

''What happened after that?'' she questioned.

''Apparently I'm as bad with money as I am at housekeeping.'' He shrugged. ''I guess I'm just not as astute financially as I should be. Anyway, I'm doing a barnstorming demonstration in Moncton at an air show on Tuesday,'' he continued, his tone becoming optimistic. ''The proceeds from that should keep my creditors at bay for a little while longer.

''Now I guess I'd better hit the sack.'' He stretched and headed for the cabin door. ''I have a charter tomorrow afternoon. I have to pick up a half dozen fishermen in Saint John and fly them to Newfoundland. Charters are my bread-and-butter work these days.''

''And the air shows, what are they?'' she asked.

''Desperation.'' He grinned ruefully. ''A

chance to make relatively big, fast bucks for a few minutes of crowd-thrilling insanity.''

''You talk as if it's extremely dangerous,'' Carol said, disturbed by his description of work which she had thought was routine for him.

''A bit,'' he said. ''But nothing I can't handle.''

''Do you have students in the morning?'' she inquired as they arose and went indoors with a sleepy beagle at their heels.

''No,'' he said, shutting the glass doors behind them. ''Not on Saturdays. I don't plan to go to the airfield until at least eleven o'clock, maybe later. If that's too late for you, you can take the Jeep and go in earlier. I have a few things I'd like to do around here first, that's all.''

''No, that will be fine,'' she said. ''The audit's coming along well. I can afford a few hours off.''

''Really? Does that in any way indicate I'm not in extremely deep trouble?'' he asked, his attempt at careless flippancy failing in his genuine concern.

She found herself confronting those wonderful sky blue eyes and her reply coming uncomfortably, necessarily from her professionalism.

''Unfortunately, no. And, really, I can't discuss it with you, Jake, not here, not now, definitely not under these conditions.''

''I understand,'' he said. ''Good night, Carol. Pleasant dreams.''

Chapter Seven

Carol awoke to the sound of birds twittering in the trees, some kind of machinery clanking, and a dog yelping joyously.

Sleepily she went to her window and pushed aside the faded curtains to see Jake wearing baggy tan shorts, an unbuttoned Hawaiian print shirt flapping out over them as he mowed the grass around the cabin with some kind of ancient manual lawn mower. The Baron was dancing ecstatically around him, barking out his pleasure in the activity. She felt a grin tugging at her lips as she turned away and headed for the bathroom. It looked like it was going to be an interesting day.

Twenty minutes later, freshly showered and

wearing a gray jogging suit and sneakers, she went to meet Jake on the front lawn.

"May I borrow your Jeep?" she asked as he paused in his mowing. "I'd like to do a little shopping in town."

"Sure." He grinned. "Think you can handle such an elegant conveyance?"

"I think so," she said. "In this line of work, I've driven so many rental vehicles, I've become fairly competent with most makes."

"Then you should have no trouble," he said. "The keys are on the refrigerator," he continued as he returned to his mowing.

A half hour later she was in the town's only supermarket and had begun to fill her cart with food and cleaning staples when she noticed two female employees in the deli department whispering and casting cold, disparaging glances in her direction. More friends of Jake's? she wondered. Friends who saw her as his new girlfriend and, therefore, their enemy?

Jake's remark about the town's water supply coming from artesian wells had made her suspicious of the Wiltsons, too. Had they been trying to drive her away? Their daughter was Jake's student. They wouldn't want Kathy to lose a chance at a promising career in aviation.

And then there was her rental car. It had been perfectly fine when she had left it in the Wiltsons' drive. The next morning after Sam Hawkins's visit to her boardinghouse, it wouldn't start and, according to the mechanic, needed major repairs. As an aircraft expert Sam Hawkins was probably knowledgeable about motors and engines of all types. He could have disabled her car in a heartbeat.

She was beginning to feel surrounded by enemies when a familiar voice ended her speculation.

"Good morning, Carol."

Turning, she saw Wade Jenkins smiling at her from behind his shopping cart. Suddenly she was inordinately glad to see him. He was the only person she had met since coming to Riverbay who wasn't a Jake Bishop fan.

"Good morning," she replied. "This must be the traditional Saturday morning activity of working people. Anyway, I'm glad we've met. I wanted to apologize to you for leaving so abruptly at noon yesterday.''

''From what I observed, you had little choice,'' he replied with a rueful smile. ''As I think I've already told you, Jake Bishop is a law unto himself.''

''But you didn't try to stop him,'' she said, bringing out the matter that had nagged in the back of her mind since the incident. ''Didn't you think I might be in serious trouble?''

''No.'' He shook his head. ''Jake has many faults, but he definitely wouldn't knowingly hurt anyone. I'll give him that much. He's just an overly macho bum, fecklessness being his greatest crime. Your shopping cart is a testament to the later charge. There probably wasn't a crumb of food in his place when you arrived. Sam told me you had moved out to Jake's cabin when I stopped by the airfield last evening to check on some insurance policies.''

''I couldn't find a place to stay.'' Carol found herself on the defensive. ''Mr. Bishop offered me the use of his spare room.''

''There's no need to explain,'' he said softly, secretively. ''I know this town.'' Then his tone returned to normal. "I'm glad we met, too. I was going to call you but I wasn't sure how Jake would react. I want to invite you to come to dinner tonight at our home. My mother, as I've told you, is an invalid and would enjoy the company."

"Thank you, I accept," Carol heard herself reply a bit too eagerly. She had been afraid of spending another lingering summer evening alone with Jake at his secluded (and for her at least), romantic cabin. "I'll ask Jake if I can borrow his Jeep."

"No need," he replied. "I'll pick you up at seven. It's impossible to keep any semblance of a civilized appearance careening about in that excuse for transportation. And I would like Mom to see you at your best."

"That's kind," she replied, but with a feeling of apprehension stealing over her. She didn't like his placing such importance on her making a good impression on his mother. The idea smacked of a seriousness of intention she wasn't prepared to accept.

"I'll see you then." Wade flashed her an engaging smile and turned his cart toward the checkout.

Jake was sitting on the steps of the small toolshed behind the cabin when she returned. He was sharpening the lawn mower blades with a file. As she got out of the Jeep, he waved and came to help her with her parcels. The Baron, who had been dozing in the sun at his feet, leaped up to gallop along beside him.

"I guess you looked into my larder and found it wanting." He grinned, picking up several bulging sacks.

"Well . . . yes." Carol hesitated, then finished with a chuckle as she gathered up an armful of bags as well.

"Actually the old place will seem a lot more like home with food around," he said as they went inside and put the bags on the kitchen table.

"It's the least I can do to repay your hospitality. Now may I impose still further? Do you mind if I do some laundry?" she asked, putting milk and margarine away in the ancient, round-cornered refrigerator. "This warm weather takes a heavy toll on cotton clothing."

"Be my guest," he said, taking an apple

from a bag and rubbing it against his gaudy shirt. "I'll restring the clothesline. Then you can hang out anything you'd prefer not to put in the dryer."

"That's not necessary," she said, closing the refrigerator and removing bread and bananas from another bag.

"No, it isn't," he said. "But I'd enjoy it. It's been too long since this house has been a home. Now that you're making it feel like one again, I realize what I've been missing. Thanks, Carol MacIntosh."

His clear blue eyes met hers for a moment before he turned and, with the Baron at his heels and munching on the apple, went out to get the rest of the groceries.

I won't get involved with you, Jake Bishop, she vowed silently as she put cleaning products under the sink and grimaced at the rubble of old, solidified ones already there. She tried to focus on her date for the evening. Wade Jenkins was tall, dark, and attractive in both appearance and personality, definitely much better suited for her career and lifestyle than a devil-may-care, financially inept, domestically disastrous stunt pilot. She didn't need the kind of complications a Jake Bishop could create in her well-organized life.

A half hour later she was tidying her bedroom while a load of clothes churned in the washer. She gathered up a pair of jeans and a navy T-shirt and decided to do a load of dark clothing later. Her frugal nature then made her wonder if Jake had any jeans or socks he needed laundered. Surely it was wasteful to run a washer only partly filled. She glanced out the window, saw him mowing the lawn down near the riverbank, and decided she didn't need to ask his permission to wash any of his jeans she found lying about.

She went into his bedroom, humming, and stopped short. The sight of a double bed centered with a tangle of sheets and blankets suddenly made her realize she was invading his privacy. She hesitated, then shrugged off her concern. She was only going to pick up a few articles of clothing to be washed. Her throwing a few pairs of socks and jeans into a washer could hardly be misconstrued as anything more than a helpful gesture.

She had finished gathering up the clothing she had decided needed laundering when she noticed a black sock hanging precariously down over the back of the big oak dresser. *I thought I'd gathered everything up,* she mused, glancing about the room. With a shrug she reached for it and was vaguely annoyed when it evaded her and dropped down behind the dresser.

"Darn!" she exclaimed, and began to tug at the heavy piece of furniture. With her penchant for detail she wasn't about to let a single, errant sock evade her.

Shortly she had moved the piece of furniture far enough from the wall to allow her to reach behind it and grope about for the sock. Her hand, however, caught something else, a piece of paper. As she removed it from its hiding place, she saw it was a newspaper clipping yellowed with age. The headline blared at her: LOCAL YOUTH SUSPECTED IN HIT-AND-RUN, and beneath, JASON BISHOP ALLEGED DRIVER OF HARLEY-DAVIDSON INVOLVED IN ACCIDENT CAUSING SERIOUS BODILY HARM.

Stunned, she read on:

On Saturday evening, a motorcycle traveling at high speed struck and seriously injured a pedestrian near the corner of Water and Pleasant streets. The victim identified the vehicle that struck her as a Harley-Davidson but failed to recognize its driver in the glare of the headlight.

The only person owning a Harley-Davidson in Riverbay is Jason (Jake) Bishop. Bishop claims his bike, which was found abandoned in a nearby field after the incident, was stolen while he was attending a local dance. No one, however, has come forward to substantiate his claim. As a result, authorities arrested Jake Bishop this morning on suspicion of leaving the scene of an accident and causing serious bodily harm.

There was a photo which showed a younger, leather-jacketed Jake being led away from the cabin in handcuffs by two burly police officers. An elderly man, gray-haired and distinguished looking, stood on the top step, his face reflecting the excruciating pain his grandson's arrest was causing him.

Carol was dumbfounded. She couldn't believe the story or the picture were real. Immersed in shock, she failed to hear Jake come into the cabin and was startled when he spoke to her from the bedroom doorway.

"So this is where you are," he said brightly. "The house looks great." Then he saw the newspaper clipping in her hands.

"I didn't know he'd kept that," he said slowly, dropping his head between his shoulders and shaking it in dismay. "Wherever did you find it?"

"I'm very sorry, I was retrieving a sock that had fallen behind the dresser, and there it was. Is it true?"

"That a woman was seriously injured by my bike? Yes. That I was riding it at the time? No." He looked up at her, his eyes full of pain. "I served a suspended sentence for it, though, and caused my granddad to have a heart attack. Not a very pretty story, is it?"

He turned and walked back out of the cabin.

Chapter Eight

Carol set lunch out on the old wooden table in a corner of the front veranda and placed two ancient lawn chairs at either end. Then she called Jake, who was raking up the grass he had mowed. He came in immediately, the Baron trotting happily behind him.

"Looks great," he said, surveying the table set for two covered with a flowered cloth and centered with a tray of sandwiches and a frosted pitcher of iced tea. "I'll wash up and be right with you."

He went into the cabin but was back shortly to pull out one of the rickety chairs for her. For all his James Dean rebel look, Jake Bishop was a gentleman of the old school and

Carol was finding the combination increasingly difficult to resist.

"I'm sorry I was abrupt earlier," he said as he sat down opposite her. "You hit a nerve with that old clipping and I responded with a knee-jerk reaction."

"Apology accepted," she said, pouring iced tea into his glass. "Even if it is unnecessary. I shouldn't have been in your room."

"Nevertheless, I'd like a chance to make up for it," he said. "Will you come on a picnic with the Baron and me tomorrow?"

He looked so little-boy eager as he shyly stretched the invitation to include the dog, Carol felt a smile tugging at her lips. He and his beagle were irresistible.

"I'd be delighted, gentlemen," she said, and bent to pat the Baron's head and set his tail thumping on the plank floor.

"I'd have asked you out to dinner tonight," he said, accepting a thick club sandwich from the tray she offered. "Only Saturday nights I have sort of standing plans."

Carol felt her heart lurch. Of course he did, she thought. Of course he had a lady friend. A gorgeous man like Jake Bishop definitely wouldn't be unattached. Why hadn't she thought of it before?

"Actually I couldn't have accepted." Her hurt and disappointment caused her to respond more quickly than she had intended. "I already have plans."

"Really?" Jake paused, the sandwich halfway to his mouth, and raised a quizzical eyebrow. "I wasn't aware you had friends in the area."

"Not really a friend," she said. "More of an acquaintance. Wade Jenkins invited me to have dinner at his home with him and his mother this evening."

"Wade again, hmm?" Jake bit into his sandwich and chewed reflectively for a moment, then continued, "Must be getting serious pretty fast, taking you home to meet his mother."

"There's nothing to get serious," Carol said softly and took a sip of her tea. "It's simply that he asked me and . . ."

"And what?" Jake stopped eating and let his wonderful blue eyes skewer her attention.

"And I don't think it's healthy for you and me to spend too many long summer evenings here alone together,'' she found herself answering honestly.

For a few moments only the sound of the river tumbling past the sun-dappled cabin beneath the birches broke the silence. Then Jake returned his attention to his lunch.

"You're right," he said, reaching for another sandwich. "Can you be ready to leave for the airfield in a half hour? I have to pick up my clients at two o'clock."

When Jake joined Carol at the Jeep thirty minutes later, she was amazed at the change in his appearance. He wore a carefully pressed tan sports shirt and pants. His brown shoes gleamed with polish. Freshly showered and with every hair brushed in place, he was the epitome of the professional charter pilot.

"What?" he asked, pausing when he caught her staring at him from the passenger seat as he started to swing into the vehicle.

"Nothing," she lied, looking quickly away.

"Right." He grinned, taking his seat and turning the key. "Go ahead and say it. You never expected me to go conventional. Well, I am a businessman, believe it or not. And," he continued, sobering, "I do take my business seriously."

"Jake, I never suggested you didn't," she protested as he spun the Jeep about and they started down the lane to the highway.

"No, but you thought it," he said, then lightened his tone and glanced over at her. "And not without justification, I might add. But now that you've seen me in my serious getup, what do you think?" He was teasing again and she knew it.

"I'm terribly, impressed," she mocked back. "Satisfied?"

"I'll have to be for now," he came back, but then continued more slowly, "until you're ready to be sincere with me."

Carol turned away and feigned interest in the countryside but actually was busy fighting down the flutter his suggestion of future involvement had started in her heart. It was a danger signal and she knew it.

Twenty minutes later she had just pulled open a full-to-bursting top drawer of a file cabinet in the airfield and was shaking her head in dismay over its tangled contents when she heard a car approaching. Glancing out

Gertie's window she saw a shiny red convertible brake to a hasty stop in the parking lot beside Jake's Jeep. A tall, slender woman, her smooth cap of dark hair cut just below her ears to reveal large silver hoop earrings, got out. She wore a short sleeveless dress that matched the color of her car and even at this distance, Carol could see the newcomer was beautiful in a svelte, magazine model way.

The woman slung the strap of a red-and-white handbag over her shoulder and strode toward where Jake was checking out his charter plane while he waited for Sam to return from lunch. The plane parked near the hanger entrance was in Carol's full view. As the woman walked briskly up to Jake, her stiletto heels clacking sharply on the pavement, Carol moved behind the file cabinet. She hated to admit it but she was suddenly curious, suddenly wanting to know who this woman was and what she wanted of Jake. She tried to lessen her guilt in hiding by telling herself that Jake knew she was there.

"Jake." The woman stopped in front of the pilot and addressed him sharply without greeting. "What is all this I hear about your being investigated?"

"Audited is the word," he said coolly. "Good afternoon, Mrs. Taylor. It's nice to see you too."

"Don't try to be smart with me, Jake!" Her face had lost a great deal of the beauty Carol had at first thought it possessed. Now it was only a hard, cold mask with green eyes glinting anger. "If this has anything to do with me, you know what I'll say. I won't change my story."

"I never expected you would," he said, running his hand over his aircraft and avoiding her outraged glare. "But I wonder what your husband would do if I told my story."

"Jake, you wouldn't!" She grabbed him by the arm and pulled him about to face her. "You promised! You know how Dave would react if he knew about you and me!"

Carol felt as if a cold steel blade had suddenly been slashed between her ribs. Jake was having, had had—the time frame didn't matter—a relationship with a married woman. She could never respect or have any feelings for a man who would do such a thing.

"Jennifer Hendricks and the Riverbay Outlaw . . . sounds like the stuff cheap novels are made of, doesn't it?" Jake faced her squarely now, blue eyes narrowing. "You're lucky I'm only in financial trouble and not aspiring to a career as a paperback novelist."

"Jake, you've got to promise me you won't say anything, no matter how this investigation goes!" She was growing desperate. "Dave is planning to enter provincial politics in the fall! The slightest hint of scandal could ruin him now!"

"I promised you once already," he said. "I've never broken my word and I don't intend to. Is that good enough for you?"

The repressed anger in his ice-cold tone would have sent shivers over a corpse, Carol thought, thankful she was not the recipient.

"I guess it will have to be." The brunet, startled by the vehemence of his words, took a step backward.

"I'm glad you're satisfied," he said, returning his attention to the aircraft. "Goodbye, Jen."

The woman hesitated, then backed away a few steps before turning and, mustering all the haughty dignity she could, strode back to her car. A moment later, with a spinning of tires, she was gone.

"Well, ask me about her."

Without turning from his examination of the plane, Jake startled Carol by addressing her.

"It . . . it really isn't any of my business," she said, coming slowly out of the office, her navy pants and yellow blouse making her feel dowdy in comparison to the woman who had just left.

"I'm not sure it isn't." His reply surprised her as he turned to face her. "And since you were probably getting an earful, it's best you ask your questions and I explain. We don't need any misunderstandings between us."

"Really, it isn't . . ." Carol was stumbling with her words.

"All right, I'll tell you," he said, annoyed at her hesitation. "Jen and I were an item back in my Harley days. And for your further information, *before* she married Dave Taylor, one of our town's leading citizens. Jen was the only girl from those times I really cared about.''

He paused and looked so squarely at Carol she wished she could shrink through the hanger floor. His honesty was almost more than she could bear.

"What happened?'' she asked, barely above a whisper.

"Jen set her cap for Dave,'' he said, turning back to the plane. "He was and always will be a sanctimonious, opportunistic bore but his family had money and position. He never would have given Jen, a relatively poor girl at the time, a second look if he'd even suspected she and I had been involved. I guess I really must have cared about her at the time because, when she asked me not to tell anyone about our relationship, I agreed. It hurt a lot but, idiot that I was, I agreed.''

"But you're telling *me*,'' Carol managed over a mouth suddenly grown chalk dry.

"You overheard. It had to be explained to you,'' he said, blue eyes boring into hers. "And,'' he continued, "you're definitely not just anyone. You need to know.''

"Why?'' She wasn't following his reasons.

"So you can better judge the character of the man you're auditing," he said. "And in case something develops between you and me."

"It won't," she managed to get out over parched lips.

"Don't be too sure, Ms. MacIntosh," he said softly, raising a hand to run its knuckles gently down her cheek. "Don't be too sure."

For a moment or an eternity (later Carol couldn't be sure which) she stood captive in his gaze. Then the sound of Sam's pickup rattling into the parking lot broke the spell and she managed to turn away and walk as quickly as weak knees would carry her back into the office.

A few minutes later as she watched from the office window as Jake took off in the King Air she was still feeling wobbly.

"Wow, Gertie!" she said softly to the busy spider. "Jake Bishop is definitely the kind of man Janice warned me about."

"There goes one great young fella." Sam, wearing soiled coveralls, came to join her, his face bright with pride. "Wouldn't mind calling him a son of mine."

"You're proud of Jake, aren't you?" Carol turned to the mechanic and decided to take the opportunity to learn more about the pilot.

"Sure am," he said, leaning on a file cabinet, ready to talk about a favorite subject. "He's done more for the troubled kids of this town than all the guidance counselors in this province could. Do you know he goes to the high school on career days and tells them about being a pilot? And he does a whole lot more. He tells them about himself and how mixed up and downright dangerous both to himself and others he was before he straightened up and got a focus on his life. When he tells how he hurt his granddad by being arrested for hit-and-run, well, let me tell you, I've seen some pretty tough kids with tears in their eyes."

"I didn't know about that," Carol said softly, impressed again by the man she was auditing.

"Yeah, well..." Sam pulled a pack of chewing gum from his pocket and offered her a stick. She shook her head and he proceeded to peel two from their foil wrappers and stuff them into his mouth before continuing.

''Then he tells 'em he's offering them the same chance his granddad offered him . . . a chance to become a really good pilot, make a decent living, and have an exciting career. He goes on to explain to them that if they can't pay, he'll make arrangements to get around the problem. I guess it's his way of trying to atone for his wild days.''

The mechanic then turned away, leaving Carol to digest what he had told her, as he ambled back to work on the Sopwith Pup.

At 6:30 that evening Carol was ready and waiting for Wade on the front steps of the cabin. She wore a navy and white ankle-length skirt and short-sleeved navy overblouse that buttoned down the back. Her golden, shoulder-length hair was loose but had been carefully trained by a curling iron into a style she felt was becoming, and although she wore little makeup, her face was bright and fresh and vibrant. She had tried to look her best but now as she discovered she was wishing Jake would come out to see the results of her efforts, she wondered for whom.

Her wish came true the next instant as Jake, fresh from a shower, stepped out of the cabin wearing tan bush pants and a green cotton sports shirt. When they had returned from the airfield an hour earlier, he had gallantly allowed her to use the bathroom first; as a result, he had been in the shower when she had finished dressing and gone out onto the steps to wait for Wade.

"Wade is a lucky man," he said. "You look great."

So do you, she thought, looking at his golden-brown hair freshly washed and brushed and looking incredibly soft and alluring in the lacy sunlight filtering down through the birches. His blue eyes seemed even bluer against his deepening tan and just as sincere and intense as ever.

"Jake." She suddenly found herself asking the question that had puzzled her since she had first seen the state of his home. "How do you manage to always have clean clothing, towels, and linen when your washer and dryer don't appear to have been used in ages until today?"

"Simple and embarrassing explanation," he said. "Erna Wiltson does my laundry in return for my giving her daughter flying lessons. George hasn't been able to work for a couple of years because of his health, but with the seasonal income from the bed-and-breakfast they've managed to make ends meet . . . just barely.

"So when Kathy decided she wanted to be a pilot, I agreed to give her lessons in return for a supply of clean laundry. I was on my way to pick some up yesterday when I found you trying to start your car. I got so involved in rescuing the damsel in distress, I forgot the reason for my trip. I'll pick it up Monday when we go in to work."

"You give flying lessons for clean laundry?" Carol could barely believe her ears. "That doesn't seem like a very profitable idea."

"Probably it isn't," he said, and changed the subject abruptly. "That outfit suits you."

"Do you really think so?" she asked, more eager for his approval than she cared to admit. "Do you really think it's okay? I wasn't sure how to dress."

"More than okay," he said, coming to join her at the foot of the steps, and Carol felt her heart suddenly thump as he stopped close behind her. She could sense his nearness so intensely she felt as fluttery as a teenager on a first date. And he wasn't even her date.

"But," he continued, moving closer, "I think these should all be buttoned."

Carol flinched as she felt his hands on her back just below her shoulder blades.

"Darn!" she managed and hoped her voice didn't sound as uncontrollably squeaky as she thought it did. "Didn't I get them all?"

She half turned, her fingers fumbling for the open buttons, but strong hands quickly covered hers, stilling her efforts.

"Allow me," he said softly, and to Carol those two polite words held all the promise of a caress.

"Oh . . . okay." She ceased her efforts but for a moment they stood as they were, his hands holding hers. And in that moment a wild romantic fantasy unfolded in her mind. She would lean back against him, against his broad chest, rest her head against his shoulder, and let his arms encircle her waist, drawing her more and more closely as he whispered in her ear. . . .

She had to pull her hands away now, before

it was too late. As smoothly and naturally as she could, she removed them and waited. She felt him push the buttons slowly through their holes, his knuckles rubbing lightly against the center curve of her back. When he had finished, he paused for a moment, fingers still on the second button, then placed his hands on her slender hips and leaned back to inspect his handiwork.

His touch sent shivers of pleasure washing over her. His hands falling so naturally onto her hips felt warm and gentle. A small sigh escaped her.

''Carol.'' Instantly he moved closer, his arms encircling her waist, her romantic fantasy of a few moments earlier becoming knee-weakening, heart-stopping reality.

''Jake, this . . . isn't . . . a good idea.'' She struggled to get out the words but his lips were brushing her temple, touching her cheek. She realized the potential explosiveness of the moment and knew she had to extricate herself immediately if she didn't want to become seriously involved with Jake Bishop. But then the scent of freshly washed hair and some

kind of heady aftershave assailed her senses
. . . and crazy things were happening to her.

"Jake . . ." His name was an anguished
gasp from her lips.

She caught at the muscular brown arms
holding her and understood why Jake Bishop
had been the idol of Riverbay's young
women. How could any woman resist his
good looks, his charm, his gentleness. . . .

Then the sound of an approaching car did
what her generally reliable cold logic had
failed to do. It gave her the strength to pull
out his embrace.

"That must be Wade," she said, busying
herself with adjusting her blouse and hair in
an attempt to avoid his eyes.

"Yes, that must be Wade," he repeated,
causing her to glance quickly in his direction
to see if there was any sarcasm intended. And
saw there wasn't. But neither was there any
hint of an apology for what he had done.

Instead he walked over to the cabin and
leaned against its weathered shingles as they
waited for the lawyer's white Cadillac to drive
out of the tree-lined lane and into the yard.

"Good evening," Wade said, and extended

his greeting to both of them with his smile as he got out of his car. "Ready, Carol? Mom's really eager to meet you."

He was wearing a casual but costly looking tan sports jacket and light-brown dress pants, only the tieless, unbuttoned neck of his snow-white shirt giving any hint of informality to the evening. A fashion model once again, Carol thought, and wondered why she wasn't impressed with his sense of style. In clothes and cars he had Jake Bishop hopelessly out-classed, and yet . . .

"A little warm for the jacket, isn't it, Wade?" Jake asked from his place by the cabin as Wade took Carol's arm to guide her around to the passenger side.

"I'm taking a lady to dinner, Jake," he said, opening her door and letting her get in. "That's something you wouldn't know much about."

"Maybe I wouldn't," Jake replied with amazing calm in view of the slur. "But it will be wise for you to remember that fact this evening."

"Jake . . ." Carol tried to protest but Wade slammed the door on her words and strode back to the driver's side, annoyance written across his handsome face.

"Hoodlum!" he muttered as he turned the key in the ignition. "Jake Bishop was and always will be just a small-town punk!"

Carol could see arguing with Wade would be pointless. Instead, she glanced in the car's side mirror as Wade angrily swung the Cadillac about, tearing up a section of Jake's painstakingly manicured lawn, to see how Jake was managing the confrontation.

The pilot was still leaning against the weather-beaten shingles of his home, hands stuffed into the pockets of his bush pants, his expression sardonic. He caught Carol's look, raised a hand in farewell, and suddenly she wished she wasn't leaving the cozy niche in the woods with Wade Jenkins. Suddenly she wished she was once again spending the evening with the pilot in his rustic retreat. But it was too late.

Chapter Nine

As she and Wade drove back toward the cabin three hours later, Carol was once again thinking about Jake. Her evening with Wade and his mother had been pleasant but she was glad it was over. Their home and lifestyle had contrasted so acutely with Jake's she felt she had been transported into an entirely different world.

The Jenkinses' home was a beautifully restored Victorian mansion furnished with lovely antiques. The dining table had been lavish and formal with fine silver, sparkling china, and snowy linen; the tossed salad, chicken Kiev, and baked Alaska served by

Wade himself excellent; and Mrs. Jenkins had proven to be a charming hostess.

As she had sat at the head of the table, the attractive silver-haired widow had impressed Carol with her warmth, dignity, and immense pride in her son. She had described him only in superlative terms: the best son a mother could have, one who had never given her anything but joy, and definitely never a moment's grief.

At that point Wade, embarrassed by her praise, had interrupted and turned the conversation to other matters. Carol thought his mother was probably right. Nothing about Wade Jenkins suggested he had ever been a troublemaker or rebel. It was the rebel part that had sent her thoughts racing eagerly back to Jake and filling her with a sense of joy at the idea of returning home to him and the Baron and the little cabin by the river.

Home. The word make her feel warm all over. She'd only stayed in the cabin twenty-four hours, yet already the word home seemed appropriate. She hoped Jake was there, back from whatever plans he had had. She glanced at her watch in the dashboard lights, saw it was only shortly after ten, and realized it was probably too early for him to have returned. After all, it was Saturday night in a small town; he probably had a date.

A date! The idea appalled her. And yet why shouldn't he take someone out? She had already told him there could never be anything between them, and he was an incredibly attractive man who had had a life before she had met him.

"You seem to be lost in thought," Wade said, breaking the silence that had grown between them for the last few minutes.

"Sorry." She forced a smile. "I do that sometimes."

"I do, too," he replied and to her chagrin, pulled the car off to the side of the road and stopped. They were in the lane leading to Jake's cabin and when he switched off the headlights, it was incredibly dark among the trees. Suddenly she didn't want to be there, alone with Wade Jenkins. Suddenly she just wanted to go home to Jake now.

"Carol, I have to talk to you," he said, turning to face her. "I'm worried about your living out here alone with Jake. There are . . . certain facts you may not be aware of in his past.''

"You mean the accident that injured a woman?'' Carol took him visibly by surprise by replying.

"He *told* you about that?''

"Yes,'' she replied. She didn't feel any need to explain it had been only after she had found the newspaper clipping. "He told me all about it.''

"And you still feel comfortable staying with a . . . a convict?'' His tone was becoming incredulous, angry.

"He served a suspended sentence for a crime he didn't commit.'' she said, hoping she could keep herself calm in the face of Wade's accusations.

"Didn't commit? He was convicted, wasn't he?''

"Courts have been wrong before,'' she said, feeling herself begin to tremble with anger.

"But not this time! You didn't know Jake back then! He was wild . . . wild and crazy! And the press had a field day with the story!

Jake looked like the stereotypical bad boy-hero right out of a movie and sported that cavalier attitude of his like he'd invented it! Hollywood was even interested in him! Just goes to show the caliber of their taste!''

"Take me home, Wade," she said, her tone making it a command not a request. "Now!"

"If that's what you want."

"I do." Carol faced straight ahead, her arms crossed stubbornly on her chest.

"Very well." He started the car with a roar and spun its wheels as he headed down the lane at a speed too fast for the narrow dirt road. "But this time next week Jake Bishop won't have a place to call home! He's about to lose everything, you know . . . airfield, aircraft, cabin, Jeep. They're all mortgaged to the hilt, and he hasn't any hope of meeting the payment due on Friday!"

"He most certainly has!" Carol countered angrily. "He's doing a barnstorming demonstration in an air show on Tuesday! He'll be able to meet his financial obligations with flying colors!"

"He thinks so, does he?" Wade swerved the car violently around a bend in the road and

Carol felt her breath knot in her throat. "Jake Bishop seems to think he's some kind of cat . . . that he'll always land on his feet. But even cats have only nine lives!"

When they drove into the cabin's yard, he braked to a violent stop. Carol was immensely relieved to see lights burning and Jake's Jeep and Sam Hawkins's pickup parked near the back steps.

"Good night," Wade said bitterly, his hands gripping the steering wheel until they were white-knuckled. He stared straight ahead. He didn't get out to open her door or offer to see her safely into the cabin. Apparently her status as a lady was gone in his opinion, she thought sardonically.

"Please thank your mother for a pleasant evening," Carol said, endeavoring to sound unperturbed by their last few minutes, although her heart was pounding with suppressed anger.

"Of course," he said, still without looking at her, and the moment she had shut the door and stepped clear of the car, gunned the motor. The Cadillac whirled about with more lawn-tearing speed, and shot off down the lane, taillights vanishing swiftly into the darkness.

Carol heaved a deep sigh of relief and headed toward the back door of the cabin. The kitchen lights shining out into the darkness were friendly and inviting even if it appeared her adversary Sam Hawkins was visiting.

She was inside the mudroom when a roar of men's laughter stopped her abruptly. That was strange. Jake must be having some sort of stag party, she thought. She hadn't anticipated anything like this. In a quandary she paused to consider her next move. There was no place else for her to go but inside and yet . . .

The Baron ended her speculation abruptly as he leaped up on the kitchen door, barking and scratching eagerly.

''What is it, boy?'' A chair scraped and before Carol could move, Jake had pulled open the door.

''Carol, hi! You're home early!'' Jake seemed genuinely pleased to see her, not in the least disgruntled by her intrusion on his evening.

Behind him, in a cloud of cigar smoke, Sam

Hawkins, George Wiltson, and another man Carol recognized as one of the two who had been joking with Sam about her at the airfield the day of her arrival sat around a kitchen table littered with glasses and snacks, cards in their hands, poker chips stacked high by each player.

"Hello." She managed to hide her astonishment and sound pleasant and unperturbed. "Gentlemen"—she nodded to Jake's guests—"I won't intrude. Please continue."

Feeling completely out of place she forced a stiff smile, then continued on across the kitchen and living room to her bedroom. Once inside her room however, she leaned back against the closed door and hugged herself gleefully. Jake hadn't had a date! His standing Saturday night plans were poker parties with his buddies! She couldn't have been happier.

Chapter Ten

She awoke the following morning to sunlight streaming in through the birches outside her window and the Baron whining pathetically outside her door.

"Coming, Baron," she said, tumbling out of bed and reaching for her robe. When she opened the door the little dog burst in joyfully, a note tied to his collar with a red ribbon.

"What . . . ?" Carol caught the beagle and read the words on the white card.

The Baron von Richthoven and Mr. Jason Bishop humbly request Miss Carol MacIntosh's presence at an elegant luncheon to be held at a secret sylvan

*location to be divulged only after accep-
tance of this invitation.*

She had to struggle to keep a smile from her lips and when she glanced up from reading the card and saw Jake waiting with little-boy anticipation stamped on his face she could suppress it no longer. She would put all financial matters on hold until Monday, she decided, knowing it probably wasn't the wisest decision but would probably produce some of the devil-may-care fun she had been craving lately.

"I'd be delighted, gentlemen," she said. "Perhaps you can tell me how one should dress for such an intriguing expedition?"

"Jeans and hiking boots." Jake broke into a grin of pure pleasure. "Definitely jeans and hiking boots."

A half hour later, Carol climbed into Jake's Jeep and patted the Baron already safely seatbelted in the back beside a large wicker picnic basket.

"Ready?" Jake asked from the driver's seat. He looked incredibly handsome in his usual white T-shirt and jeans. He took a pair of sunglasses from the dash and put them on.

"Ready for takeoff, Captain," she replied, reaching into the glove compartment to find her glasses. Forty minutes later she was realizing her flippant remark.

Lunch, beagle, man, and young woman were ensconced in Jake's Piper Cub and cruising down the runway, rapidly gathering the speed required for takeoff.

"Jake, this is crazy, totally crazy!" she cried above the noise of the engine. "No one takes an airplane to a picnic!"

"Don't they?" He grinned at her from behind his sunglasses. "We apparently do."

"Why?" she asked.

"Because, as you said, taking an airplane to a picnic is crazy and you seem like a lady who is due to be allowed to be a little crazy."

Carol thought of Gertie endlessly spinning her webs and never going anywhere.

"You're right," she said, and laughed as the Baron, seated behind her, managed to stretch far enough forward in his restraint to lick her ear.

Then she gave herself over to the complete

joy of the flight. She had flown many times but always in large aircraft which generally offered conditions not unlike those of the living room of her Toronto apartment with nothing to see but clouds, darkness, or a blazing, unrelenting sun. This was entirely different.

Below, a breathtaking vista of trees, meadows, and lakes spread out like a microcosm of all that was best and natural in the world. And when they left the last of the small farms and their outbuildings behind and proceeded over what appeared to be pristine wilderness, Carol felt no apprehension, only the thrill of being involved in a wonderful adventure with a thoroughly intriguing man. She understood now what Jake had meant about the little aircraft giving a true sense of the magic of flight. She was light-headed with happiness, excitement, and anticipation. It was going to be a great day.

"Are you having a good time?" Jake asked once about fifteen minutes into the flight.

"I'm having a terrific time, thank you." She smiled over at him.

"Good," he said. "I was sure you possessed a little of your Irish grandmother's thirst for adventure. Now I think it's time we got to that picnic. I have a feeling the Baron's getting hungry and that will never do.''

He pointed ahead to indicate a large lake glistening in the summer sun. ''There's a pier at one end. I'll land and we can have our lunch on the lawn of a cabin nearby. It belongs to the Wiltsons. They're not staying there this weekend so we'll have the place all to ourselves.''

The plane began its heart-stopping descent. To Carol it seemed the water of the lake was rushing up to meet them. Her hands were white-knuckled as she clung to the seat, her heart seemingly lodged squarely in the back of her throat.

Then they were down and skimming over the water. Jake had landed the aircraft so smoothly she had felt only a slight lurch as they had made contact with the lake's calm surface.

''Wow!'' she cried, and burst out laughing in sheer exhilaration. ''That was great!''

Jake, involved in taxiing the plane up to a dock, was grinning broadly at her enthusiasm.

Two hours later Carol sat on the verdant

grass beneath a spreading maple tree in front of the log cabin on a rise above the lake and clasped her arms about her drawn-up knees. Besides her, on a blanket, the remains of their meal had been stored away in containers; on the other side of the picnic cloth, Jake lay stretched on his back, using his arms behind his head as a pillow, seemingly asleep. Beside him lay the Baron still gnawing on his own special lunch treat, a large roast beef bone.

Carol gazed out over the lake watching a pair of loons, young ones on the mother's back, float peacefully past. She remembered the wonderful hamburgers Jake had grilled on the Wiltsons' big old-fashioned stone barbecue and how good they had tasted in the wilderness air washed down with the iced tea Jake had brought in a tall thermos. The peacefulness of the place pervaded her senses and she sighed in pure delight.

Then a frown slowly began to shadow her expression. The perfection of the scenario faded as she realized a fact she could no longer deny. She was definitely falling in love with Jake Bishop. It wouldn't work, but now she must allow herself to admit the reality.

And, she thought, brightening a little, for the next few days, the next few wonderful days, she would revel in that knowledge. Later she would deal with the pain of having to leave him.

But before she got to the agony of parting from him, she would have to do her best for him. She would have to find a way to save his beloved airfield. And she thought she just might be able to. An idea had come to her as she had been gazing out at the lake and the more she pondered it, the more she believed it could be a viable solution.

"Jake?" she asked softly, wondering if he was really asleep.

"Ummm?" he replied drowsily.

"Have you ever thought of applying for government assistance for your airfield?"

"What did you say?" he asked, coming slowly to a sitting position, and there was no warmth in his tone.

"I was just wondering if you'd ever applied for government assistance," she said, his tone and expression making her apprehensive.

"Is that what you think of me and my business?" he said, tone and expression hardening. ''That I'm so poor I need welfare? Well, let me tell you, *Ms.* MacIntosh, Bob Bishop never took any government handouts and neither will I!''

''That's not what I meant.'' Carol struggled to keep a level tone before blue eyes that were suddenly as hard and icy as sapphires. ''I was thinking in terms of having your flying school classified as a government-accredited post-secondary institution. That way it gets official acceptance both professionally and financially.''

The hardness in Jake's expression began to soften into interest as she explained.

''It could help the kids a lot, couldn't it?'' he said.

''It certainly could,'' she said. ''It would give you more time to concentrate on them since you wouldn't have to perform those ka-mikaze stunts at air shows or fly as many charters.''

''That's right,'' he said, eagerness for her idea coming into his tone. ''I could take on more students and concentrate more of my time on them. That would be great! But,'' he continued, his enthusiasm taking a downturn,

"I wouldn't know how to go about it. I wouldn't know where to begin."

"But I do!" Carol went over to kneel beside him, her face bright. "I've dealt with government agencies all of my professional life! I can do it for you! Our agency actually has an 'in' with your provincial government. The Angus MacDonald Accounting Agency has just recently saved them millions by exposing a bogus computer training facility."

"But would that be ethical?" he asked. "Aren't you supposed to be getting all the facts necessary to close me down?"

"No, of course not!" She was astonished at his lack of comprehension of her function. "I'm only here to gather the facts about your actual financial status. That definitely doesn't preclude my offering viable possibilities that might improve your prospects. In fact, I'm sure the firm that presently holds your mortgage would much prefer you stayed in business. I'm sure they'd have no use for an airfield relatively distant from heavily populated areas."

"Are you certain?" Jake looked at her sharply. "There was a rumor—"

"Of course I'm certain." Carol had had

enough of his misconceptions for one day. "First thing tomorrow I'll make a few phone calls, get the proper forms, generally start the ball rolling."

She was vibrant with enthusiasm as she knelt before him, but suddenly she saw the expression in his eyes changing. She could not even pretend she didn't know what it meant nor that she would have changed it if she could. And when Jake moved slowly forward to touch her lips lightly with his, she could not deny she went as weak and weightless as if she had been touched by magic.

Then just as slowly he moved away. "This isn't a good idea," he muttered as much to himself as to her. "Not a good idea at all. Not now, at least while you're still auditing me and especially not while you're staying at my place. Last evening told us that much, didn't it?"

Their eyes met and her logical accountant's mind knew he was right even if her heart, body, and soul didn't.

"You're right," she said, her tone far too bright to be sincere, and scrambled to her feet. "We'd better be getting back, don't you think?"

Chapter Eleven

Early Monday morning Carol was hard at work in the airfield office. She totaled the numbers of hours Jake spent with students each week, how many were able to pay for their lessons and how many weren't, how many hours more Jake could devote to instruction if he were freed of the necessity of performing in air shows and taking on too many charters, and exactly how much financial support was needed to keep the airfield operational. Then she began making telephone calls.

Finally she managed to reach the deputy minister for whom her firm had recently worked in uncovering the computer training scam. When she began to outline her ideas for the airfield, he seemed only mildly interested but as she continued to talk, he became caught up in her enthusiasm and started to ask questions. Finally, he declared he saw no reason why such an operation should not receive assistance.

"The Provincial Department of Education has actually been trying to come up with some sort of postsecondary institution in that area for young people who can't afford to attend universities or other training facilities farther afield than their immediate area," he said. "This flight school sounds like just the ticket, one of its kind in the region, and offering a training program which will suit students for careers pertinent to today's job market. I'll have to check with a few other people but I think you can rest assured of our assistance. I'll call you at seven o'clock this evening with confirmation."

"I'd be grateful," Carol said, suppressing the sigh of relief that was being held in check at the back of her throat.

"Any institution recommended as a solid investment whether in financial terms or in its benefit to the economy of a region by the Angus Mac Donald Accounting Agency has to be worthwhile,'' he said, and Carol silently prayed he was right.

She was putting not only her own professional reputation on the line but also that of her agency. And without Janice Nickerson's knowledge or consent. Even though her CEO had empowered Carol to act on the firm's behalf Carol knew her employer had not meant to the extent of using its name and reputation to obtain financing for a failing airfield operated by a convicted felon.

Then came a lurch in her smoothly moving plan.

''Could you repeat the name of the gentleman who owns the field?'' the government official asked, apparently involved in taking down information.

''Jason Bishop,'' she replied, keeping her fingers so tightly crossed they hurt and begging all the powers of the universe not to let the name set off any alarm bells.

''*Jason* Bishop, hmmm.'' The voice on the other end of the telephone grew contemplative. ''The name sounds vaguely familiar.''

Then it once more came up to speed. "Couldn't have been in any matter of importance, otherwise I'd remember. I'll call you this evening, Ms. MacIntosh. And thanks for offering this most suitable suggestion."

He hung up and Carol was left with a general sense of accomplishment heavily seasoned with searing trepidations. What if the deputy minister found out about Jake's past? Her agency could be charged with promoting a coverup. Its business license could be withdrawn, its reputation destroyed. Abruptly she stopped speculating. The terrible possibilities suddenly seemed endless.

"I've really put my foot in it big time, Gertie," she said, crossing the room to confide in the only creature she could trust at the moment. "If this goes belly up . . ."

Then Jake appeared in the office doorway, his arm draped about the shoulders of the tough-looking young man who had come for flying lessons on Carol's second day at the airfield. Carol felt a hot surge of embarassment shoot through her veins. *I hope he didn't overhear me talking to Gertie!*

"Guess who just soloed?" Jake was grinning almost as broadly as his companion. "Guess who's going to make one heck of an airline pilot someday soon?"

"Terrific!" Carol felt Jake's immense sense of accomplishment reach out and catch her up in it. "Zack, that's just terrific."

Apparently Jake and Zack had both been too immersed in their accomplishment to have been listening to her ridiculous conversation, she thought with an inward sigh of relief.

"Yeah, well, it is kind of cool." Zack shifted from one foot to the other, embarrassed by the praise but at the same time basking in it. "I'll see you guys later," he continued and turned to leave. "I think I'll go and tell my old man." Then he sauntered as casually as his eagerness would allow him out of the hangar. Through Gertie's window Carol saw him burst into a run once he thought he was out of their sight, leap onto his bicycle, and head toward the highway at record speed.

"Six months ago, Zack was into shoplifting big time and had just stolen his first car." Jake came to stand beside her and watch him go. "He and his father weren't even on speaking terms. His mother was at her wits' end. Now . . .''

''That's wonderful, Jake,'' she said, looking at Gertie resting in one corner of the window. ''And I have more good news. It looks as if you're going to get the funding you need. A deputy minister is going to call us this evening at the cabin with confirmation.''

''You managed to do all that . . . this morning?'' Amazement took possession of Jake's expression.

''Actually it was largely luck,'' she said. ''I just happened to offer a solution to a problem their department was currently confronting.'' She wasn't about to make him feel indebted by telling him the extent to which she had to commit her agency and her own career.

She started to turn away from the window but he had been standing so close to her she ended up facing him a mere inches away from those provocative blue eyes.

''Thanks anyway,'' he said softly, his voice deepening with emotion.

''It was nothing.'' She tried to be casual as she averted her eyes and tried to slip past him, her heart racing.

"Don't," he said, catching her by the shoulders. "Don't keep denying what's between us. I can see it in your eyes; I can feel it when we touch. Admit it, Carol. You care for me as much as I care for you."

Then he was kissing her gently, tentatively at first, then so intensely Carol felt as if she were flying again, soaring high and free over a totally wonderful world.

For the moment, nothing else mattered, only Jake's strong arms holding her, only his lips on hers, only the strength of an attraction so powerful she knew she could never forget or deny it.

She also knew she loved, would always love Jake Bishop, even when they weren't together anymore, even when she went back to her office in Toronto, her own special kind of web.

"Jake." With an effort that nearly wrenched her heart from her chest, she put her hands against him and pushed away from him. "We're only hurting each other with this. We both know . . ."

"Oh, yeah, right!" He released her and for the first time Carol caught a flash of the bel-

ligerent tough guy who had been so hurt by
his parents' apparent preference for his
brother he'd rebelled. Love and its lacking
meant a lot to Jake Bishop, she realized. "For
a minute I forgot ours is strictly a business
arrangement. Please forgive me if I've over-
stepped the boundaries of our professional relationship. I have to get back to work
anyway." He turned and started out of the office. "I have a gig in an air show tomorrow.
I want to make sure the Pup is up to it . . . just
in case this guy of yours doesn't come
through."

"He will. . . ." Carol tried to reassure him
but he was out of the office and striding
through the hangar toward the biplane. She
felt sick and lost and hollow, completely hollow. She knew she had hurt him deeply. He
didn't deserve it, she thought. Jake Bishop
was a good man. But what choice did she
have?

A charter client called just as she and Jake
were about to leave for home at 5:00 that afternoon. He wanted complicated arrangements
made in order to pick up several of his friends
for a fishing trip. He and Jake had to have

several telephone conversations over the next forty-five minutes, with the customer calling Jake and then his friends, and then Jake again, and then his friends. When the couple finally locked up and drove away from the airfield it was nearly 6:00.

''The Baron won't be pleased,'' Jake said as he shifted gears and headed out onto the highway. ''He's accustomed to eating promptly at five-thirty.''

He seemed to have put their moment of intimacy and its unpleasant aftermath out of his mind. Carol was relieved yet saddened. She didn't want him completely shutting it out . . . or her . . . ever.

''I asked Sam to pick up a couple of steaks and a bottle of red wine,'' she said, trying to draw her mind away from the matter. ''We can have a celebratory supper as soon as we get that call from the deputy minister.'' She indicated bags in the back of the Jeep and Jake nodded, without his usual grin, in her direction.

''Sounds good. We have to eat even if he never calls.''

''He will,'' Carol replied cheerfully, but felt

a little of Jake's pessimism brush over her. She shivered and pulled her linen cardigan more securely about her shoulders. She must not let his feelings of rejection, feelings for which she knew she was responsible, cloud her skies just now.

The Baron met them at the door, full of haughty disdain. After a lukewarm greeting, he trotted imperiously over to the cupboard that housed his dog food and stood looking up at Jake with all the commanding insolence of an absolute monarch.

"Okay, okay." Jake gathered up food and water bowls from the floor and proceeded to fill both.

In the time it took him to care for the beagle, Carol put the wine in the refrigerator, placed the steaks in a low pan, and poured a marinade over them. Then she turned to her companion and forced a smile.

"There. Now I think I'll get out of this dress and into a pair of jeans. Will you listen for the telephone? He might call early, although I doubt it. He was most precise about seven o'clock."

"Yeah, okay." Jake took a beer from the

refrigerator, snapped it open, and went to sprawl in one of the living room chairs.

"Jake, I'm sorry," she tried to placate him. "But we both know . . ."

"Yeah, sure, no problem." He waved aside her attempt to explain and gathered up the Baron who, with his hunger satiated, had come to join them, tail wagging.

Just before she closed her bedroom door, Carol glanced back at the pair and saw Jake holding his little dog in his arms, gently stroking its velvety ears.

How can I? she thought, furious with herself. *How can I hurt such a terrific man?* Yet she could see no alternative. She was a professional, not some starry-eyed teenager ready to drop everything and become domestic simply because a gorgeous man had kissed her, albeit with a magic and intensity she'd never known. No, she had worked too hard to become a Chartered Accountant to throw it all away for a crazy, head-spinning, stomach-lurching sensation called love.

Chapter Twelve

It was 10:30. Thunder rumbled from a distance and beyond the glow of two lamps on living-room end tables, the cabin and its surroundings were bathed in hot, sultry darkness. The telephone call hadn't come.

Carol brushed a damp strand of hair back from her burning forehead and felt a tension headache beginning above her left eye. She couldn't believe it. The deputy minister had been so positive her proposal would pass muster.

"Jake, I don't know what could have happened," she began apologetically as they sat on the porch swing. "It seemed like such a done deal."

"It doesn't surprise me," he said, bitterness tainting his tone. "These government guys are generally just a lot of hot air. It's no big deal. I've managed on my own all along and I will continue to do it."

She caught the double meaning in his words and flinched inwardly.

"Jake, you know I care for you but it won't work. You're a client; I have a job to do. . . ."

"Yes, I know," he snapped back, and took another sip of the wine he had been drinking. "You're a professional, a lady with a stellar career of making innocent people look like embezzlers!"

"Jake, that's not fair!" she cried, jumping to her feet. "I'm only doing my job, I'm . . ."

"You're only costing me my airfield, my granddad's raison d'être!" he yelled, and suddenly the air between them was as statically charged as the storm-ripe atmosphere hovering above them.

"I'm not costing you anything!" she yelled back, infuriated by his accusation. "You're responsible for your businesses' deplorable state! You and your Saturday-night poker games!"

"What!?"

A bolt of lightning lit up the sky. In its glare, she saw the raw outrage on his face.

"You heard me!" she bellowed above the ensuing thunder.

Both were now on their feet, facing each other in unleashed pain and anger.

"You gamble! That's why you have no money, that's why you've got receipts for airplane fuel that was never expended on recorded flights!"

"Oh, so you found that, did you?" He seemed to be towering over her now but Carol MacIntosh, C. A. was not about to be intimidated. "After seeing my friends here on Saturday night you put the two facts together and decided that, in view of my past, I was perfectly capable of falsifying my business records to cover my gambling debts!"

"Well, how would you explain it?" She glared up at him, desperately hoping she wouldn't cave in under those arctic blue eyes that were bombarding her with icy shards of outrage.

"Lessons for students who can't pay!" he snapped. "With all of your financial insights and training, I would have thought that would have been obvious to you. Especially after you met Zack. And I do have records I keep myself. I have to keep track of every hour those kids fly in order for them to get their licenses. I keep their logs here at the cabin so I can work on them at night! They're my best-kept accounts because they're so important! As for the gambling, have you ever heard of penny ante . . . playing for pennies? Well, that's exactly what we do on Saturday nights! Real dangerous back room stuff, right?''

With that he turned and strode into the cabin. Carol watched as the bathroom door slammed behind him. A moment later she heard the shower. A cold shower, she presumed.

Slowly she turned, went into her bedroom, and prepared for bed. The thunder and lightning had gone as quickly as they had come but now rain thundered down on the cabin in a bitter assault. As she listened to it bucketing over the weathered shingles, she saw Jake's face again in her mind and the terrible pain and anger in his blue eyes was more than she could bear.

Twice she started to get up, to go to him, to try to make him listen while she explained, but each time told herself it would be no use. She had hurt him too deeply for words to mend. She would be leaving in a few days anyway, so what difference did it make? she tried to tell herself. Soon Jake Bishop would be only a memory, and there was a list of things she would remember about him.

She would remember, for example, that he was strictly a toast and coffee man at breakfast, that he liked old movies and vintage country music, that blue was his favorite color, medium-rare steak with mushrooms, green peppers, and onions his favorite food. She knew that he loved aircraft of all kinds and peace and quiet and small dogs. . . .

She also knew there was a lot about him she would give a great deal to have the time to learn. Did he often sit before a crackling log fire in the big stone hearth on winter evenings? Would he enjoy her grandmother's recipes for seafood casserole and carrot cake? Did he hate formal attire as much as she did? Did he snore . . . ?

She stopped abruptly. Two tears were trickling down her cheeks. Carol MacIntosh, Chartered Accountant, was crying.

She awoke the next morning to the sound of Jake's Jeep gunning out of the yard. She sat bolt upright. He was leaving without her! Instantly she was scrambling out of bed and into her robe.

In the kitchen she found the Baron leisurely licking the last of his breakfast from his bowl. A note from Jake told her tersely that he had to leave early because of the air show and that Sam would pick her up later.

Carol shuddered when she thought of Jake performing those death-defying stunts in that vintage aircraft replica. Probably still angry and hurting from their quarrel, he was not in any condition for such a concentration-demanding activity. Carol shivered and understood how his grandmother must have felt when Robert Bishop had been flying that same aircraft. If only that call had come.

After she had showered, dressed in a white blouse and casual beige pants (she couldn't bring herself to dress like a professional that day), and forced down toast and coffee, she went out onto the steps to wait for Sam. Suddenly she remembered she was supposed to have called Baycom yesterday with a progress report. With all that had been happening, she had forgotten.

I can do it while I'm waiting for Sam, she thought, glancing at her watch. *It will only take a few minutes. I'll simply tell them I'll send them a full report by courier later this week.*

With the Baron prancing along behind her she returned to the living room and picked up the telephone. There was no dial tone.

"What in the world . . . ?" she began, then saw that the wire leading to the jack behind a chair looked unnaturally limp. Suspicious, she gave it a flip. A raw, chewed end flew into view.

"Baron, you chewed through the telephone wire!" she cried. "You got tired of waiting for Jake to come home and feed you, so you chewed through the connection! No wonder we didn't get a call! Maybe . . . probably he did call and couldn't get through! Probably Jake doesn't have to do that air show! Oh, Sam, hurry up!"

As if in answer to her plea she heard Sam's

pickup coming down the lane to the house and shortly they were on their way to the airfield. The moment they arrived, Carol saw that Jake's Sopwith Pup was gone. Desperate to learn the outcome of her negotiations yesterday, she raced across the hangar, flung her purse and briefcase aside, and began punching the assistant deputy minister's number into the telephone. After three rings a secretary answered and upon learning who was calling immediately put Carol through to the man she wanted desperately to speak to.

"Ms. MacIntosh?" His tone was cordial. "I tried many times to reach you last evening but there seemed to be a problem with that number you gave me."

"Yes, actually there was," she said, not going into details. "I am sorry."

"No problem." The voice was again warm and friendly. "I merely wanted to confirm your client will get government support, with both financing and certification."

"Thank you." Carol had to struggle to quell her natural response which was to shout, "Great! Terrific! Wonderful!" Instead she continued with professional calm, "I won't forget your support."

"Any business that appears as highly viable to the Angus Mac Donald Accounting Agency as this one obviously does is a sure thing in our books," he replied. "Now I'm needed on the other line. The paperwork will be on its way to you today. Good luck."

He hung up and Carol almost simultaneously dropped the receiver back into its cradle.

"Sam!" she yelled out the office door into the hangar.

The mechanic, beginning to work on Jake's Piper Cub, turned, surprised at her unladylike outburst.

"We got a government grant! Jake doesn't have to fly in that air show!"

"What did you say?" Sam turned to her, puzzled. "What grant?"

"Oh, that's right, you didn't know we'd applied for one." Carol quickly went on to explain.

"Well, now, isn't that something!" Sam was grinning by the time she had finished. "I was real worried about the boy. He didn't give me time to check the Pup out this morning.

He was more concerned that I go pick you up, I guess.''

''How can we stop Jake from flying in that show?'' Carol asked. ''We have to hurry!''

''Call the terminal building in Moncton . . . the number's on the cover of the office telephone book. They can probably make radio contact with him.''

Five minutes later Carol leaned back in the captain's chair behind the scarred old desk and breathed a sigh of relief. She had telephoned the airport where Jake was performing and they had assured her they would contact him immediately with her news. Humming a little tune, she went over to a coffeemaker she had unearthed from beneath piles of paper on Saturday afternoon and had cleaned to a usable state.

''Would you like a cup of coffee, Sam?'' she called out to the man who had returned to working on the Piper Cub. ''I got in touch with the airport. They're going to contact Jake, so we can relax.''

''Sounds good, Miss.'' He came to stand in the office doorway, wiping his hands on a rag. ''Bob, Jake's granddad, always made coffee in the mornings. Sometimes I'd stop at the bakery in town and buy a few doughnuts to go along with it. But Jake doesn't have much of a domestic streak in him so we've lost our ten o'clock coffee.''

"Well, in celebration of the turnabout in finances, let's have a coffee break." Carol grinned, raising a still empty mug to Sam. "Tomorrow we'll have doughnuts to go along with it."

Chuckling inwardly at Sam's remark about Jake's lack of domesticity, she turned away from the mechanic's deepening smile and began to put coffee and water into the machine. Wouldn't he have been surprised if he had seen his boss mowing his lawn dressed like a typical suburban husband on a Saturday morning or repairing a sagging clothesline or barbecuing hamburgers and making iced tea?

Sam knew only the macho, devil-may-care good old boy Jake he saw around the airfield; he didn't know the full depth and scope of the man he called "Boss" as she did. She knew the real reason Jake hadn't kept up his grandfather's coffee breaks was because he couldn't spare the time; he had to work every waking minute to keep his business afloat.

Fifteen minutes later as she and Sam were sipping coffee in the office Carol saw through Gertie's window a familiar white Cadillac driving into the airfield parking lot. Shortly Wade Jenkins walked into the hangar. There he stopped short and stared at the place reserved for Jake's Sopwith Pup.

"Where's the Pup?" he asked without greeting the pair as they came out of the office.

"Jake's using her in an air show this morning . . ." Sam began.

"No, he can't be!" Wade's tanned face sallowed with horror. "He couldn't have gotten it off the ground . . . he . . ."

"What are you talkin' about, Jenkins?" Sam put his coffee mug down on a workbench and started menacingly toward the attorney.

"I . . . I knew that if Jake didn't get the money from performing in the air show today, he'd fail to meet a crucial payment and lose the field," he stammered. "So I came out here last night and disabled the Sopwith Pup. I don't see how he could have gotten it off the ground with two parts missing!''

"Two parts!" Sam's weathered face hardened with rage. ''What two parts?''

"I don't know! I don't know anything about aircraft! I just got into the cockpit and pulled a couple of pieces out!'' Wade Jenkins was clearly terrified. ''I thought they'd make it impossible for him to fly at all!''

"Describe them!" Sam ordered tersely, his lean jaw working with a nervous tick.

Wade gave a shaky, detailed description and Sam swore under this breath.

"What does it mean?" Carol caught the mechanic desperately by the arm.

"It means Jake probably has no radio capabilities and could start to lose altitude at any moment,'' the mechanic muttered, staring at the terrified lawyer, his face hardened like stone with anger. ''If anything happens to that boy, Wade Jenkins, I'll see you rot in prison!''

"I didn't . . . mean . . . I . . .'' Wade Jenkins sank onto a greasy workbench unmindful of his pale gray suit.

"Never mind all that!" Carol took control of the situation. ''We've got to call Moncton

... see if they can get Jake down immediately! Maybe they can use semaphore if all radio transmission is out!''

She raced into the office and grabbed the telephone.

Five minutes later she walked slowly back into the hangar where Sam and Wade Jenkins waited.

''They can't reach him,'' she said faintly, numb with terror. ''He's already performing and his radio is out.''

Ten minutes later the office telephone rang, its high-pitched cries raking over Carol's raw nerves. She half dashed, half stumbled to it. Wade and Sam, who had followed her, saw her face blanch as she listened, then wordlessly replace the receiver on its cradle.

''Jake's crashed,'' she said tonelessly. ''He was trying to land and his plane crashed on the end of the runway. Emergency crews are on the scene now.''

Chapter Thirteen

"Get into my truck!" Sam was grabbing her by the arm and propelling her out of the hangar. "We're going to Moncton . . . *now!*"

Carol was barely aware of being thrust into the passenger seat of Sam's pickup or of seeing a ghastly looking young lawyer standing frozen in horror at the hangar door in the rearview mirror as they roared away. Her heart and life seemed to have stopped, frozen in a terrible place called dread.

The two-hour drive to the city seemed interminable. Sam, ashen-faced and silent, drove as fast his old truck could go and still avoid the highway patrol. Carol felt alternately nauseous and floating, bathed in a sense of unreality at the unthinkable possibility that she may have to face. She knew now that she couldn't leave Jake. Ever. She loved him utterly, completely. Life would be a meaningless void without him. She'd stay forever; she'd be his accountant; she'd run the financial end of his business; she'd cook his meals and wash his socks and feed his eccentric little beagle; she'd . . .

But what if there is no Jake to care for, to care about? a horrific little voice inside her grated. *What if . . .*

Carol clutched the armrest until her fingernails left scars in the paper-thin upholstery. *No, please no!* She shut her eyes and prayed silently.

After they had identified themselves to airport security, they were immediately taken to a deserted VIP lounge to await an official who would inform them of the details of the crash.

From a window Carol saw the Sopwith Pup being towed from the runway, one wing hanging limp and broken like a wounded bird. Its propeller was smashed back toward the cockpit.

"Sam . . . !" Carol clutched at the mechanic's arm.

"Easy, Carol, easy." He called her by her first name for the first time and patted her slender, manicured fingers with his gnarled, oil-stained ones. "I've seen pilots walk away from a lot worse." But she felt the tremor running through him.

"Miss MacIntosh? Mr. Hawkins?" An airport official wearing a short-sleeved white shirt, black tie and dress pants stepped briskly into the lounge and closed the door after him.

"Jake . . . ?" was all Carol could manage at that point.

"He'll be up shortly," the man easily, as if nothing had happened. "He's clearing away some paperwork."

"He's all right?" Carol felt her knees go weak and leaned heavily against Sam's bony shoulder.

"Aside from bruised ribs, I believe so," he replied and smiled. "It could have been a lot worse."

"Yes, it certainly could have been," she breathed, watching the Sopwith Pup vanish out of sight around a hangar behind a tow truck.

"Hi, guys."

Jake stepped into the room and grinned at the pair as if nothing untoward had happened.

"Jake!" Carol took a couple of steps toward him, then her legs failed her. She knew one more move and she would collapse. Relief as intense as this was more than she could handle.

"Carol, honey." Instantly he was beside her putting his arms around her and helping her to a couch. When they were seated, he looked up at Sam, his left arm around Carol's shoulders, and extended his right hand to the mechanic. "Good to see you, buddy." He grinned.

"Good to see you, too, Boss." Sam grasped Jake's proffered hand and shook it vigorously, a grin splitting his gaunt face from ear to ear. "Good to see you, too."

"Jake, are you really all right?" Carol found her voice again to ask.

"Sure," he said, looking down at her with such loving tenderness it made her heart flutter uncontrollably. "But it would have been a lot worse if a certain accountant I know hadn't suggested using semaphore to bring me down.''

At that moment the door burst open and Wade Jenkins stumbled into the room. His face was death pallored and he was trembling violently.

"Jake!" he choked when he saw the pilot and slumped against the doorframe. "Thank goodness!"

"Wade, what's wrong?" Jake was instantly on his feet and going to assist the lawyer into a chair. "You look like you've just seen a ghost, man."

"He probably thinks he has." Sam advanced toward the pair, thin hands knotted into fists at his sides. "He tried to kill you, Jake."

"No, not as God is my witness, I never meant to do that!" Wade's hands were shaking so violently he could barely pull a handkerchief from his pocket to wipe sweat from his forehead and upper lip.

"Tell me," Jake said gently and put an arm about the lawyer's quaking shoulders.

"Yes . . . I'll tell you." Wade Jenkins sank

into a chair, his hands shaking violently. "It's time . . . time I got rid of all those lies . . . time . . ."

He covered his face with his hands. It was several minutes before he was sufficiently composed to begin his story.

On the Saturday night of the accident, Jake had left his bike unattended with the key in the ignition outside the local dance hall. Wade had seen it and a plan had begun to form in his mind. During the dance, when Jake had gone out into the meadow behind the hall with a girl . . . here Wade glanced quickly at Carol, trying to gauge her reaction to this bit of information, but she managed to appear involved in Wade's story . . . he had seized the opportunity. He would take a quick ride on Jake's bike before Jake and the girl came back to the dance. It would be the thrill of his life.

"I . . . I'd always envied Jake," the lawyer confessed brokenly, staring down at his shaking hands clutched close to his face as he sat with his head hanging in shame. "I wanted to be like him . . . own a Harley, have girls chasing me . . . be a rebel. But Mother wouldn't let me ride on a motorcycle let alone own one.

And in school, I was always the smart one, the kind no girl would give the time of day. But that night I saw my chance to be like Jake . . . just for a little while." He paused and looked at Carol, then continued slowly, heavily, "I was driving the Harley when it hit that woman," he choked, breaking down. "And all these years I've let Jake take the blame . . . because I was jealous of him, hated him for being all the things I'm not."

"No!" Carol breathed. She hadn't expected such a poignant revelation.

"It could easily have been me, Wade," Jake said softly. "I drove crazy in those days. The accident and its consequences brought me to my senses. Fortunately I had a great old guy for a grandfather. He saw me through the whole mess. And it was then I realized I owed it not only to him but to myself to wise up. I sold the Harley and went to work for him at the airfield, first getting my pilot's license, and then helping him teach kids, especially those who appeared headed for trouble, to do the same."

"You knew, didn't you, Jake?" Wade asked brokenly. "I saw you come running around the corner of the dance hall in the seconds between my starting the engine and actually pulling out of the parking lot. You recognized me and yet you never told anyone. Why?''

''Because, as I've said, it could well have been me, but mainly because of your mother,'' Jake astonished Carol by replying. ''She admires you, Wade, loves and admires you the way I've always wished my mother loved me. I couldn't destroy anything that terrific by letting her know her son was involved in that kind of accident. You see, while you were envying me, I was envying you. And it was an accident, no matter who was driving the bike. No one meant to hurt that woman.''

''But the girl you were with,'' Carol couldn't help but break in. ''She knew the truth. Why didn't she come forward?''

The three men exchanged glances, then Jake explained slowly, carefully.

''Back in those days, some of the most *respectable* girls in town thought it was cool to be involved with the village bad boy,'' he said, looking unflinchingly at Carol. ''But none of them wanted their parents or, in some cases, their *real* boyfriends to know. The girl I was with in the meadow that night was definitely one of the above. I think she'd have faced death rather than fess up to being with me at the time of the accident.''

"She should have, though," Sam muttered. "If she had had a shred of conscience, she would have. And now she's married to the mayor."

Jake grinned ruefully at Carol. "Even back in those days, our town's present first lady had her eye on the up-and-comer who later became our mayor. A young man with political ambitions would not have been overjoyed to learn his intended was spending time with the likes of me. I wasn't about to ruin her chances. You see, at the time, I thought I was in love with her."

"Jennifer," Carol breathed, remembering the tall, slender brunet who had to come to see Jake at the airfield on Saturday morning to secure his promise of silence because she believed he was being personally investigated.

"Jennifer," he nodded, his tone deepening into one of remembrance.

"But why did you try to kill Jake now, after

all these years?'' Carol asked, turning to Wade. She had to change the subject. She couldn't think of Jake with that beautiful, cold creature. She just couldn't.

''I didn't try to kill him!'' Wade jumped to his feet and strode across the room to stare out at the runway. ''I only wanted to disable the Sopwith Pup so he couldn't fly in the air show and would default on his mortgage payment. I am . . . was working for Baycom, a consortium that wants to buy the airfield, demolish it, construct a youth correctional center, and then lease it to the federal government. The flat tableland of Bishop's Airfield is excellent for such a facility . . . escapees could be seen for miles on that vast, cleared acreage. Baycom offered me a job in Toronto with a salary that would allow me to hire a full-time companion for my mother if I succeeded. It would have been my ticket out of here, away from the guilt.''

''Baycom!'' Carol was appalled. ''You mean we're both working for the same company? Now I understand why James Caremore was so eager to have our firm do the audit on Bishop's Airfield! It would give the closure legitimacy and cover up any nefarious acts you committed on their behalf! Janice Nickerson will be furious when she learns this! James Caremore will be made to live up to his surname very quickly once she gets to him!''

''I shouldn't have gotten involved,'' the lawyer muttered. ''I'm out of my league with those people. I almost killed a man to achieve their ends. I can't believe it!'' He shuddered and shook his head in disbelief.

''Wade, it's over.'' Jake arose and went to put a hand on his quaking shoulder. ''And it's high time you started over . . . as the good man you can be. Stay in Riverbay. Look after your mother. Help me with my legalities and any of my kids who occasionally need counsel. It's not a bad life. There's lots of people in Riverbay who can use a good attorney, an affordable attorney.''

''You're still willing to trust me . . . after this?'' Wade Jenkins looked incredulously at Jake.

''Why not?'' the pilot shrugged. ''People trust me to have changed. Now I'll trust you to do the same.''

Chapter Fourteen

As they drove back to Riverbay in Sam's pickup, Sam cleared his throat uneasily.

"I owe you an apology, Carol," the mechanic said.

"What!" Jake exclaimed in pretended astonishment. "Sam Never-Say-I'm-Sorry Hawkins is about to apologize? I've got to hear this!"

Sam shot Jake a withering look, then continued, "I was the reason you couldn't get a place to stay in town, the reason your car wouldn't start."

"I suspected something like that," she murmured.

"I thought you were out to close Jake

178

down,'' he continued, hurrying to explain. ''I couldn't think of any other way to prevent your doing it. And when I told people about you, about what I thought you were planning to do, they were more than willing to help drive you out of town. Jake has a lot of friends in Riverbay.''

''Especially the Wiltsons,'' Carol said softly. ''Taking my room from me seemed so very painful for them.''

''Jake's been a big help to them with Kathy,'' Sam surprised her by explaining.

''Come on, Sam. Carol doesn't need to hear all that,'' Jake cut in but his friend was determined.

''Yes, she does, Jake,'' he said. ''It's important that Carol understand just what kind of a man you are. Kathy Wiltson ran away from home a little over a year ago, Carol, with a young fellow who was in trouble with the law. Erna and George were at their wits' end to know what to do. Well, the long and short of it, Jake helped track Kathy down and then went to see her. He told her about his own past, including how it had hurt his grandfather and how he wished he had a chance to live those years over again. Kathy listened and finally decided she didn't want what had happened to Jake and his grandfather to happen to her and her parents so she came home.

"Jake introduced her to Danny Matheson, a real nice young man, and they've been a couple for over a year now. Oh, Kathy has a big crush on Jake but both of them know it for what it is and have it under control. It doesn't hurt that she still looks up to him and takes his advice, though."

"So you felt they owed Jake one and you collected," Carol said, her tone reflecting her distaste for such a course of action.

"Yeah." Sam looked ashamed. "Yeah, I did, there's no denying it, but"—he glanced defiantly in her direction—"I'd do it again if I had to . . . for the boss."

Jake lowered his head, shaking it slowly. "Sam, I don't know whether to be moved to tears or give you a good, swift kick in the rear. Your intentions were the best but you almost cost me the woman I love."

At first Carol couldn't believe she had heard correctly. Was Jake actually saying he loved her for the first time, as they bounced along in the hot, dusty cab of an ancient pickup, as she sat between him and his mechanic? She couldn't imagine anything less romantic ... or more sincerely open and honest.

"I realize that." Sam continued concentrating on his driving, apparently not surprised by Jake's matter-of-fact declaration. "But"— and here he glanced at Carol, his face crinkling into a grin—"I didn't, did I, Carol?"

"I ... I ..." She looked from the mechanic to Jake and saw his eyes had grown softly intense, a smile vibrant with tenderness and caring on his lips.

"Pull over at that picnic site up ahead, will you, buddy?" Still smiling with such caring that Carol felt herself drawn immediately, tenderly, wonderfully, irrevocably into his heart, Jake put a hand over Carol's. "Carol and I need a few minutes alone."

"Sure." Sam was grinning broadly. "I'll just take a cat nap. It's been a rough day ... up until now."

A few minutes later Jake, his arm about Carol's shoulders, stopped at a bend in a trail behind the picnic site and turned her to face him.

"I love you, Carol MacIntosh," he said softly. "And I apologize for the way I made the declaration back there in the truck. You deserve a much more romantic moment than that. But the fact has been so well established in my heart for so long, I guess I didn't think it was necessary to inform you. I thought you must have known. Certainly my emotions got involved on that first day at the airfield when I wiped that smudge from your nose. You were such a beautiful, warm, loving little creature and yet you were trying so hard to be a cold, detached professional I couldn't resist you. You were struggling to keep your feet on the ground but your heart was in the clouds. 'This is not self-centered Jennifer Hendricks or ice-cold Captain Molly Bishop,' I told myself. 'This is the kind of woman I want to share my life.'

"And when your dress did a Marilyn Monroe imitation . . . well, I was hopelessly hooked," he finished, his eyes dancing with mischief.

"I might have guessed," she teased back. "Strictly an animal attraction."

"Yeah, right," he said, sobering and gazing deep into her eyes. "An animal attraction that involves the entire heart and soul of one aging, former rebel. Think you can handle it, Madame Accountant?"

"Just try me," she breathed, and he kissed the tip of her nose, a smile so full of love and caring crinkling his eyes and mouth it brought tears of joy to her eyes. Then he drew her tenderly into his arms.

"But Jake," she asked softly a moment later against his shoulder. "What about your granddad? It was extremely unselfish for you to protect Wade, his mother, and Jennifer but you hurt one of the people you loved most in the world in the process."

"Granddad knew the whole truth," he startled her by replying. "And at first he tried to convince me to tell it, to make Jen and Wade confess. But I refused. That hit-and-run had made me come to my senses. In all likelihood, it would have been me riding that bike that night. It would have been me that hit that woman. I'd take the heat I deserved and when

I got out from under the consequences, I would make some drastic changes in my lifestyle.''

He paused but Carol pressed him on.

''If you and your granddad shared the truth and an agreement as to the outcome, why was he so traumatized as to have a heart attack?''

''The media,'' he said hoarsely. ''Granddad hadn't counted on the coverage the story would get. You saw only one example. I guess the incident made good copy because it was everywhere for a while . . . TV, newspapers, radio, the works. Shortly afterward I even got an offer to stunt double in a movie, would you believe.'' He shook his head in disbelief.

''I can understand,'' Carol said, softly touching his cheek. ''A handsome supposed outlaw like you . . . you would have been terrific movie and publicity material.''

''Yeah, well, it all turned out to be too much for Granddad. Seeing me in handcuffs in newspapers and being shoved into police cars on TV was more than he could stand. One night when we were watching an item on the late news where a police officer had me up against a patrol car, hands on the roof, feet spread, Granddad just slumped over with a massive coronary. He never fully recovered.''

For a moment he rested his forehead on Carol's shoulder and she let him have his remembrance of grief.

Then he looked up at her and smiled. ''Granddad would have liked you,'' he said softly. ''He would have told me I'd better marry that girl and be quick about it. And that's exactly what I plan to do . . . even if she does confide in spiders.''

''Jake . . .'' she tried to gasp out her chagrin but he cut it off as he kissed her, and suddenly it was the Fourth of July with clear blue skies and fireworks and not a single snowflake in sight.